The Hackman Story

The Descendants of Henry Hackman of Lancaster County, Pennsylvania

By Dorothy Elaine Grace
& Lawrence Knor

The Hackman Story
Copyright © 1976, 2010, by Dorothy Elaine Grace
and Lawrence Knorr.
Cover copyright © 2013 by Sunbury Press, Inc.

For information about special discounts for bulk purchases, please contact Sunbury Press, Inc. Wholesale Dept. at (855) 338-8359 or orders@sunburypress.com.

To request one of our authors for speaking engagements or book signings, please contact Sunbury Press, Inc. Publicity Dept. at publicity@sunburypress.com.

SECOND SUNBURY PRESS EDITION
Printed in the United States of America
February 2013

Trade paperback ISBN: 978-1-62006-188-6

Published by:
Sunbury Press
Mechanicsburg, PA
www.sunburypress.com

Mechanicsburg, Pennsylvania   USA

Dedication

With Love to my Cousins,

It is my hope that by reading this story of your ancestors, you will develop a greater appreciation and understanding of those intangible traits and attitudes, which have become part of you. Then, too, I hope that you will become more fully aware of the fact that fine people in all generations find life a combination of joy and sorrow, understanding and misunderstanding, success and failure– tempered by love. An abundance of love has come to you, handed down from generation to generation. It has not always been understood by those directly involved. There have been many "hurts," but love's bond is strong and enduring. It is the substance of which special men and women are made. This book is dedicated to you, one of the grandchildren of a very special man, Henry Hess Hackman.

Lovingly,

Dorothy Elaine Hackman Grace
1976

Contents

Earliest Hackmans

The earliest Hackmans we found are listed in *Pennsylvania German Pioneers*[1]. Peter Hackman arrived in Philadelphia on 16 October 1727, and on the same ship was Jacob Heistandt. On 11 September 1731, Jacob Hackman (age 20) and Johan Heistand (age 19) arrived in Philadelphia on board the same ship. This is interesting because Jacob Heistandt's family intermarried with the Hackman family. Elizabeth (age 25) and Rudollf Hackman (age 20) docked on 1 September 1725. On 2 September 1749, Ulerich Hackman and Johannes Hackman arrived on the same ship. One might assume that Ulerich and Johannes knew each other before they sailed. They had even been related. Henrich Hackman (age 22) arrived on 15 September 1753. Abraham Hackman arrived on 30 September 1754, and Jacob Hackman arrived on 21 October 1761. It is difficult to determine which, if any, of these pioneers were the actual ancestors of the Hackmans as we know them today.

There are five Hackmans listed in the 1790 census. The first census figures were not too accurate; consequently, there were undoubtedly Hackmans who were not included in the census figures. The Hackmans who were included in the 1790 census are as follows:

Henry Hackman – His family consisted of one free white male of 16 years and upward, two free

---

1   Ralph Beaver Strassburger, LL.D., *Pennsylvania German Pioneers,* William John Hinke, Ph.D., D.D. (Baltimore: Genealogical Publishing Co., Inc., 1975), Volume I.

white males under 16 years, and three free white females. These figures suggest that Henry and his wife may have had two sons under 16 and two daughters (no indication of their ages) in 1790. They were located in Conestoga Township, Lancaster County, Pennsylvania.

Melchor Hackman – Also in Conestoga Township was Melchor Hackman's family, which consisted of two free white males of 16 years and upward, and four free white females. Melchor and his wife may have had one son (over 16) and three daughters. One cannot assume that these individuals were family members. For instance, there may have been farm workers, relatives, or friends living with the family.

Ulrich Hackman – lived in Mount Joy Township, Lancaster County, Pennsylvania. His family consisted of one free white male of 16 years and upward (this would have been Ulrich, himself), and one free white female who was probably his wife or an unmarried daughter or sister.

Henry Hackman – Another Henry Hackman was located in Warwick Township, Lancaster County, Pennsylvania. We believe that this Henry is our direct ancestor. Henry sold his land, in 1792, to his son, Jacob Hackman[2] It seems a valid assumption that in the 1790 census Henry Hackman was listed as the head of the household with his son, Jacob, being the other male over 16. According to the deed, Henry's second wife, Ann, was deceased by 1789. She would not have been included in the census. Jacob Hackman is not listed in the 1790 census. Yet, he should have had a family by that time. It is quite feasible that the two males under 16 were his

---

2   Lancaster County Deed R 6 392, Henry Hackman to Jacob
    Hackman, Lancaster County Courthouse, Lancaster,
    Pennsylvania.

sons, and the three females were his wife and two daughters.

John Hackman – The last Hackman listed in the 1790 Census is John Hackman. His family consisted of two free white males of 16 years and upward, two free white males under 16 years, and three free white females. This family settled in Montgomery County, Pennsylvania.

Another source of early information is the Lancaster County Courthouse in Lancaster, Pennsylvania. Again, from this information one can venture educated guesses. Ulrich Hackman of Mount Joy Township, Lancaster County, Pennsylvania, in his will, probated 18 April 1797, appointed his brother, Henry Hackman of Warwick Township, and Frederick Mumma of Donegal Township, as his executors[3] Peter Heistand and Christian Martin witnessed this will. Abraham Hackman of Cocalico Township, Lancaster County, Pennsylvania, in his will, probated 6 February 1765, writes, "I select of this my last will my two loving friends and brothers of law executors viz Henry Hackman and Abraham Brubaker"[4] We cannot tell if this is the same Henry Hackman or if Ulrich, Abraham, and Henry Hackman were brothers. It seems clear, however, that Ulrich Hackman of Mount Joy Township and Henry Hackman of Warwick Township were brothers.

---

3   Ulrich Hackman will, X 2 307, Lancaster County Courthouse, Lancaster, Pennsylvania.

4   Abraham Hackman will, Z 2 296, Lancaster County Courthouse, Lancaster, Pennsylvania.

Generation I

Henry Hackman of Warwick Township, Lancaster County, Pennsylvania, is the earliest ancestor we can confidently claim. We do not know who his first wife was, however, his second wife was Ann Histand, the widow of Jacob Histand.[5] Jacob and Ann Histand had issue: John Histand, the eldest son, Mary Histand, Elizabeth Histand, Abraham Histand, Ann Histand and Jacob Histand, who died intestate, unmarried and in his minority.

On 16 April 1792, Henry Hackman (now referred to asHenryHackman,Sr.), sold his farm in Warwick Township, consisting of 69 acres, 80 perches and bordering the lands of Andrew Wissler, John Groff, Martin Whiteman, Peter Elser, and Rudolph Bollinger, to his son, Jacob Hackman, for a consideration of "600 pounds in gold or silver coin."[6] This tract of land had passed from Jacob and Mary Everly on 3 May 1753 to Jacob Histand who died intestate leaving a widow Ann and issue as mentioned before. John Histand sold the land to Henry Hackman, Sr. The release was signed 18 April 1789. In 1789, Henry Hackman, Sr. had married Ann Histand, and she was deceased. This deed, written in 1792, is the last record we have of Henry Hackman, Sr. We do not know where he is

---

5   Henry Hackman to Jacob Hackman deed, R 6 392, Lancaster County Courthouse, Lancaster, Pennsylvania.

6   Henry Hackman to Jacob Hackman deed, R 6 392, Lancaster County Courthouse, Lancaster, Pennsylvania.

buried. We cannot find a will. We assume that since he is referred to as Henry Hackman, Sr., he must have had, in addition to Jacob, a son, Henry. There undoubtedly were other sons and/or daughters.

Henry Hackman, Sr., had issue: Jacob Hackman and Henry Hackman.

Generation II

Jacob Hackman of Warwick Township, Lancaster County, and Jacob Hackman of Elizabeth Township, Lancaster County, are one and the same. The description and history of the land are identical in the deed from Henry Hackman to Jacob Hackman and in the deed transferring the same land from Jacob Hackman to John Brubaker. The earlier deed, although written after Elizabeth Township was formed from Warwick, lists the township as Warwick. The more recent deed places the property in Elizabeth Township.[7]

Jacob Hackman was married to Elizabeth Heistand.[8] Elizabeth Heistand's brothers and sisters were: Peter married to Hannah, Magdelena married to Michael Little, John, Jacob, and Barbara married to Peter Erb.[9] By December 1820, Peter, John, Jacob and Barbara were all deceased.

In his will, Jacob Hackman makes no reference to his wife; consequently, it is assumed that she predeceased him. He indicated "my son-in-law, John Brubaker shall have the option of buying the part of said plantation which he now has".[10] We cannot be completely sure where Jacob Hackman

7   Jacob Hackman to John Brubaker deed, Q 6 58, 20 May 1829, Recorded 13 January 1840, Lancaster County Courthouse, Lancaster, Pennsylvania.
8   Jacob Heistand will, I 1 24, Lancaster County Courthouse, Lancaster, Pennsylvania.
9   Misc. Book 1816-1822, December 1820, page 547, Lancaster County Courthouse, Lancaster, Pennsylvania.

and his wife are buried although we believe that markers inscribed 'Grandmother Hackman and Grandfather Hackman' and placed in the Hammercreek Mennonite Church Cemetery by their grandson, Andrew Hackman, were meant to be a memorial to them. They may or may not actually be buried there.

---

10 Jacob Hackman will S 1 358, 5 November 1839, Lancaster
    County Courthouse, Lancaster, Pennsylvania.

Jacob Hackman's Will[11]

In the name of God, Amen. I, Jacob Hackman, Senior, of Elizabeth Township in the County of Lancaster and state of Pennsylvania yeoman, being old in perfect health of body and sound mind memory and understanding (praised be God for the same) but considering the uncertainty of this transitory life do make and publish this my last will and testament in manner and form following to wit:

First it is my will and I do order that all my just debts and funeral expenses be duly paid and satisfied as soon as conveniently can be after my decease.

Item, it is my will and I do order that all my personal estate shall be sold at public venue excepting my wearing apparel, as soon as conveniently can be after my decease.

Item, I give and bequeath unto my sons, Jacob Hackman and John Hackman and unto the children of my deceased sons Henry Hackman and David Hackman all my wearing apparel so as my son Jacob gets one share thereof, my son John gets one share thereof, the children of my deceased son Henry gets one share thereof and the children of my deceased son David gets one share thereof.

Item, it is my will and I do order and direct that all my plantation and tract of land whereon I no live

11 Jacob Hackman will S 1 358, written 5 November 1839, Probated 30 November 1840, Lancaster County Courthouse, Lancaster, Pennsylvania.

situate in Elizabeth Township in the County of Lancaster, adjoining the land of Jacob Wissler, Peter Elser, and others containing by my estimation about sixty-four acres be the same more or less shall be sold at public venue as soon as conveniently may be after my decease for cash by my hereinafter named Executors to such person or persons and for such price or prices as may be reasonably gotten for the same and if my son-in-law John Brubaker agrees to take the part of said plantation which he now has in use and included at the same price as the other will fetch for cash he may have it, but if he doth not contract with my said Executors to take the same before the day of sale then it shall be sold with the other land and for that purpose I do hereby authorize and empower my said Executors or the survivor of them to sign, seal, execute and acknowledge all such deed or deeds of conveyance as may be requisite and necessary for the granting and issuing the same to the purchaser or purchasers thereof (and the said John Brubaker if taken by him as aforesaid) in fee simple.

Item, it is my will that out of the monies arising from the sale of my personal and real estate my children shall be made all equal with the adjustments I have written down, and I have given to each of them in my life time, and after my deceased children and my children now alive are made equal then the balance of the monies remaining out of my personal and real estate shall be made in eight equal shares. One equal share thereof I give and bequeath unto my son Jacob, one equal share thereof I give and bequeath unto my son John, one equal share thereof I give and bequeath unto the children of my deceased son Henry, one equal share thereof I give and bequeath unto the children of my deceased son David, one equal share thereof I give and bequeath unto my daughter Nancy, one equal share thereof I give and bequeath unto my daughter Elizabeth, one equal share thereof I give and bequeath unto the children of my deceased daughter Catharine.

Item, it is my will and I order and direct my said Executors to sell by public venue all my tract of wood land for cash situate in Elizabeth Township aforesaid adjoining to land of Peter Stauffer, John Brubaker, and others containing five acres be the same more or less to such person or persons and for such price or prices as may be reasonably gotten for the same as soon as conveniently can be after my decease and for that purpose I do hereby authorize and empower my said Executors or the survivor of them to sign, seal, execute, and acknowledge all such deed or deeds conveyance as may be requisite and necessary for the granting and issuing the same to the purchaser or purchasers thereof in fee simple and the money arising thereof to be paid by my said Executors unto my eight children aforesaid.

Item, it is my will and I order and direct my said Executors to sell by private or public sale all my tract of land situate in the province of Upper Canada containing three hundred and fifty acres to such person or persons and for such price or prices as may be reasonably gotten for the same for cash after my decease and for that purpose I do hereby authorize and empower my said Executors or the survivors of them to sign, seal, execute and acknowledge all such deed or deeds of conveyance as may be requisite and necessary for granting and issuing the same to the purchaser or purchasers thereof in fee simple, and the money arising thereof to be paid by my said Executors unto my eight children as aforesaid. And lastly I nominate and appoint my son Jacob Hackman and my neighbor Christian Risser of Elizabeth Township to be the Executors of this my will hereby revoking all other wills, legacies and bequests by me heretofore made,

*and declaring this and no other to be my last will
and testament.*

*In witness whereof I the said Jacob Hackman,
Senior have hereunto set my hand and seal the fifth
day of November Anno Domini one thousand eight
hundred and thirty-nine.*

Jacob Hackman had issue:

Jacob Hackman (Jacob Hackman appears so
often in Hackman genealogy we cannot determine
which Jacob is the son of Jacob of Warwick or
Elizabeth Townships.);

John, who was the executor of his father's will
and guardian of two of his deceased brother, David's
children;

Henry, deceased on 30 November 1840, married
Maria Snavely;

David, born 21 September 1801, deceased 29
December, 1831, married Susanna Bear;

Nancy, born 6 December 1788 and died 21
November 1862. Her husband, John Gingrich, son
of Joseph Gingrich, was born 12 March 1788 and
died 26 November 1831.[12] who in the will is listed as
one of the eight children of Jacob Hackman
(however, no Nancy signed the release – it seems
likely that the Anna Gingrich, widow, of Waterloo,
District of Wellington, Province of Canada, who
signed the release is the former Nancy – her father
Jacob Hackman had 360 acres of land in Upper
Canada).[13]

Elizabeth, married John Erb[14],

12 Eby, Ezra E., *A Biographical History of Early Settlers and
Their Descendants in Waterloo Township*, compiled 1895 &
1896, page 171. Descendants of John and Anna Gingrich are
included on pages 171 and 172.

13 Release, Jacob Hackman heirs to executors, Deed Book X 6 29,
Lancaster County Courthouse, Lancaster, Pennsylvania.

Maria, married to Abraham Musselman who was appointed the guardian for her children (she was deceased by the time the will was probated[15], and Catherine, who married John Brubaker. She was also deceased by 30 November 1840, when the will was probated.[16]

---

14 Release, Jacob Hackman heirs to executors, Deed Book W 6 149, Lancaster County Courthouse, Lancaster, Pennsylvania.
15 Ibid.
16 Release, Jacob Hackman heirs to executors, Deed Book W 6 149, Lancaster County Courthouse, Lancaster, Pennsylvania.

Generation III

We believe that the second son, John, married Maria Mussleman and lived, at least for a time, in Lebanon County.[17] A Maria Hackman "born Musselman" is buried in the Hammercreek Mennonite Church Cemetery next to the graves of some other Hackman family members. There is no husband buried with her.

The third son, Henry, married Maria Snavely, daughter of John Schnebely, Sr., of Heidelberg Township, Lebanon County, Pennsylvania.[18] Henry was born 4 June 1786, and died 28 June 1831.[19] Maria was born 2 June 1788 and, and died 23 June 1849.[20] Both Henry and Maria were said to be buried on the Horst Brothers' Farm, one mile east of Schaefferstown, Lebanon County, Pennsylvania.[21] However, when we visited there, we found Maria's gravestone and the stones for her parents. Henry's stone was not there. We did not ask at the farm. Perhaps the stone fell over and was removed. The private cemetery is well-kept. We know that this is the Henry, son of Jacob of Elizabeth Township,

17 Lebanon County Deeds G 474 and E 553, Lebanon County Courthouse, Lebanon, Pennsylvania.
18 John Schnebely will, B661, 1842, Lebanon County Courthouse, Lebanon, Pennsylvania.
19 News clippings, etc., Snavely-Heistand-Hackman folder at State Library, Harrisburg, Dauphin County, Pennsylvania.
20 Personal visit to cemetery.
21 Snavely-Heistand-Hackman folder at State Library, Harrisburg, Dauphin County, Pennsylvania.

Lancaster County, for several reasons. First, Noah Hackman (born 1815) "the son of Henry"[22] signed the release in 1842 for the will of Jacob Hackman (Henry's father) of Elizabeth Township.[23] Henry Royer also signed the release. Henry Royer was named the guardian for the minor children of Henry Hackman at the time of his death.[24] Henry Royer was married to Maria Snavely Hackman's sister, Catharine.[25] In addition to these facts, Henry's brother David named Henry as one of his executors.[26] The will was written 3 January 1831. It was probated 18 February 1832. Between the time the will was written and the time it was probated, Henry died.[27]

Henry Hackman and Maria Snavely Hackman had issue:[28]

Noah Hackman, born 22 February 1815, buried at Peru, Illinois;

David Hackman, born 12 May 1817, died 29 April 1836, buried at Horst Farm, one mile east of

---

22 Lebanon County Orphans Court record E 91, 1841, Lebanon, Pennsylvania.

23 Release Jacob Hackman heirs to executors, 6 149, signed 1 April 1842, recorded 23 May 1842, Lancaster County Courthouse, Lancaster, Pennsylvania.

24 Lebanon County Orphans Court record E 91, 1841, Lebanon, Pennsylvania.

25 Jacob Schnebely will B 661, 1842, Lebanon County Courthouse, Lebanon, Pennsylvania.

26 David Hackman will Q 1 179, Lancaster County Courthouse, Lancaster, Pennsylvania.

27 Ibid.

28 Snavely-Heistand-Hackman folder at State Library, Harrisburg, Pennsylvania. I could not verify this information; however, various Lebanon County Courthouse records seem to indicate that it is accurate. Will B 142, Misc. Books C 365, C 648, C 367.

Schaefferstown, Pennsylvania (we did not see this grave when we were there);

Elizabeth Hackman, born 12 December 1819, died (in the cradle) 28 June 1826, buried one mile east of Schaefferstown, Pennsylvania. (We did not see this grave.);

Maria (Mary) Hackman, born 7 March 1822, married Benjamin Ream, buried in Peru City Cemetery, Peru, Illinois;

Lydia Hackman, born 6 October 1824, married Willie Oberholtzer or Overholtzer, died in the east;

Henry Hackman born 1 March 1828, buried in Peru City Cemetery, Peru, Illinois;

Elizabeth Hackman, born 29 November 1830, married Henry Ream, brother of Benjamin Ream in 1857, died one year later, buried in Miller Cemetery, north of Spring Valley, Hall Township, Bureau County, Illinois – no issue – This is the second Elizabeth, the first one having died.

David Hackman (son of Jacob) married Susanna Frantz Bear.[29] We traced Susanna's genealogy in Appendix A. She was the daughter of Johannes Bear and Anna Frantz Bear.[30][31]

David and Susanna Hackman lived in Elizabeth Township, Lancaster County, Pennsylvania. We believe that they were in this area as late as 10 April 1830, when five- month-old baby, Anna, died. She is buried in the Hammercreek Mennonite Church Cemetery. The back of the tombstone says "Rebuilt by A.B. Hackman, bro., 5 July 1913."

Family tradition says that David Hackman became partially frozen while driving a Conestoga

29 John Bear petition to sell property. Misc Book 1827, page 392, Lancaster County Courthouse, Lancaster, Pennsylvania.

30 Orphans Court Records 1827, page 392, Lancaster County Courthouse, Lancaster, Pennsylvania.

31 Anna Bear will, U 1 953, Lancaster County Courthouse, Lancaster, Pennsylvania.

wagon between Philadelphia and Sunbury.[32] He died at the early age of thirty on 29 December 1831.[33] David was buried in the Becker private family cemetery in Rapho Township, Lancaster County, Pennsylvania. In his will[34] he refers to the the land in Rapho Township that he is purchasing from Mrs. Groff. We believe that sometime between 10 April 1830, when baby Anna died, and 29 December 1831, when David died, the family moved to Rapho Township. We have been unable to find any land records for David Hackman in Rapho Township. It is interesting to note that although the Hackman family completely left Rapho Township, David Hackman's great grandson, Henry Hackman, one hundred years later, met and married Minnie Becker, the great granddaughter of Jacob Becker. Henry and Minnie reared their family on the Becker farm, which had been handed down from generation to generation in the Becker family, and on which both of their great grandparents were buried.

After her husband's untimely death, Susanna sought guardians for her three surviving children.[35] The petition is as follows:

To the honorable Walter Franklin, Esquire, president and his associate judges of the Court of General Quarter Justices of the Peace in and for the County of Lancaster comprising and presiding an orphans court for said county.

The petition of Susanna Hackman widow relict of David Hackman late of Rapho Township in said

---

32 Henry H. Hackman interview, September, 1976.
33 Gravestone, Millport Mennonite Cemetery, Warwick Township, Lancaster County, Pennsylvania.
34 David Hackman will, Q 1 179, Lancaster County Courthouse, Lancaster, Pennsylvania.
35 Petition for guardians, Misc. Book 1831-1833, page 461, Lancaster County Courthouse, Lancaster, Pennsylvania.

county yeoman deceased humbly says that said deceased left issue three children to wit Jacob Hackman, David Hackman, Andrew Hackman, all of whom are minors under the age of fourteen years for whom no guardians have been appointed over their persons and estates. Your petitioner therefore prays your honors to appoint Henry Neslie of Elizabeth Township, yeoman, guardian over the person and estate of the said Jacob Hackman and John Hackman of the same place guardian over the persons and estates of said David Hackman and Andrew Hackman during their minority and she will pray.

15 April A.D. 1833

David Hackman's Will[36]

In the name of God, Amen! I, David Hackman, of Elizabeth Township in the county of Lancaster and State of Pennsylvania, yeoman, being weak in body, but of sound mind, memory and understanding,

36 David Hackman will, Q 1 179, Lancaster County Courthouse, Lancaster, Pennsylvania. The will-book copy is typed. The lines and blanks included here appear in the will-book copy.

blessed be God for the same, but considering the uncertainty of this transitory life, do make and publish this my last will and testament. In manner and form following to wit.

Principally and first of all, I command my immortal soul, into the hands_____ who gave it, and my body to the earth to be buried in _____ decent and Christian life manner, at the discretion of my executors hereafter named.

Item, I give and bequeath unto my beloved wife Susanna, two large beds and bedsteads, and the small bed and bedstead, one table, one chest, one bureau, one stove, one spinning wheel and reel, four chairs, the kitchen dresser, and as much kitchen furniture, as will be necessary for her use, and all the linen and liney in my possession, and as much salted meat as she thinks to be in need of, and my silver watch. And it is my will and I order and direct that the remainder of my personal property shall be sold at public sale by my said executors as soon as conveniently may be after my decease.

Item, it is my will and I order and direct that my executors herein after named, or the survivor of them, shall as soon as conveniently may be after my decease, sell and dispose of the plantation which I bought of Mrs. Groff, per agreement, situate in Rapho Township, Lancaster County, to such person or persons, and for such price or prices, as may be reasonably gotten for the same, at public or private sale for cash, or the one half in hand, and the remainder in two yearly payments as they think best, and for that purpose, I do hereby authorize and empower my said executors, or the survivor of them to sign, seal, execute, acknowledge all such deed or deeds of conveyances as may be requisite and necessary for the granting and assuring the same, to the purchaser or purchasers thereof, in fee simple.

Item, it is my will and I order and direct my executors hereinafter named, or the survivor of them, to purchase a house and lot of ground on a convenient place for the use of my wife, during her natural life, or as long as she remains my widow after my decease. And after her decease or day of marriage; it is my will that the said house and lot of ground shall be sold by my said executors or the survivor of them for the use of my estate at public or private sale for cash, and I do hereby authorize and empower my said executors or the survivor of them to execute a good and lawful deed or deeds of conveyance for the same, to the purchaser or purchasers thereof.

Item, it is my will, that after my just debts are all paid and the house and lot of ground as aforesaid, the the one third part of the money arising or left out of my personal and real estate, shall be and remain in the hands of my said executors or the survivor of them, and they shall put it out on interest with good security, and they shall pay the interest thereof, yearly, unto my wife, during her natural life, or until the day of her marriage after my decease; and the remaining two thirds part of the money arising or aforesaid, I give and bequeath unto my children in equal share to be divided between them, or their assigns, according to law, to be paid out.

Item, I give and bequeath also unto my children, the one third remaining in the hands of my executors as aforesaid, and the money arising from the house and lot of ground as aforesaid, in equal shares to be divided between them or their assigns, to be paid to them after the decease of my wife as aforesaid.

And lastly, I nominate, constitute, and appoint John Frantz, a brother to my mother-in-law, and my brother Henry Hackman, to be executors of this my will, hereby revoking all other wills, legacies, and *bequests by me heretofore made, and declaring this and no other, my last will and testament.*

In witness whereof, I have hereunto set my hand and seal, the third day of January, anno domini, one thousand eight hundred and thirty-one.

Witnessed by Peter Elser and Samuel Eberly

David Hackman was buried in the Becker family cemetery, Rapho Township, Lancaster County, Pennsylvania. In 1976 the farm was operated by John Hackman, the son of Henry H. Hackman and Minnie Becker Hackman. The stone was rebuilt and relocated in 1915, by Andrew B. Hackman, the son of David Hackman. He placed the stone in the Millport Cemetery where other Hackman family members are buried. He placed a duplicated stone in the Becker cemetery where David is actually buried. Pictured below is the original stone which was rebuilt and moved to Millport.

David Hackman and Susanna Bear Hackman had issue:

Jacob Bear Hackman, born 26 March 1825, died on 20 January 1899, married Maria, born on 26 August 1830, died on 9 May 1897. Both buried in Hammercreek Cemetery, Lancaster County, Pennsylvania.[37]

David Bear Hackman, born on 19 May 1827, died on 16 November 1896, married (1) Harriet B. Miller, born on 5 February 1829, died on 9 December 1870, and (2) Ella Caroline Gabel[38], born on 26 April 1851, died on 2 February 1907. All

37 Gravestones, Hammercreek Cemetery.
38 Knorr, Lawrence & David Baer Hackman, *A Pennsylvania Mennonite and the California Gold Rush: The Journal and Letters of David Baer Hackman* (New Kingstown, PA, Sunbury Press, Inc., 2008), page 212.

David Bear (or Baer) Hackman (1827 - 1896)

three are buried in Manheim Borough Fairview Cemetery, Manheim, Lancaster County, Pennsylvania.[39]

Andrew Bear Hackman, born 5 July 1828, died 27 July 1916, married Martha Eschbach Brenner, born 15 February 1839, died 17 July 1913[40.] She was the daughter of Jacob Brenner and Susanna Eschbach Brenner. Andrew and Martha are buried

---

39 Gravestone, Fairview Cemetery located in Manheim, Lancaster County, Pennsylvania. Additional evidence concerning Ella is found in the 1880 Census.

40 Gravestones, Millport Cemetery, Warwick Township, Lancaster County, Pennsylvania, and Family Bible held by Martha Hess Hackman, published 1835. The gravestone clearly indicates Martha died 11 July. The Bible shows 17 July.

in the Millport Cemetery, Warwick Township, Lancaster County, Pennsylvania.

Anna Hackman, born 27 November 1829, died 10 April 1830, buried in the Hammercreek Church Cemetery, Lancaster County, Pennsylvania.[41]

106 N. QUEEN ST.
LANCASTER, PA

Andrew Bear (or Baer) Hackman (1828 - 1916)

---

41 Gravestone, Hammercreek Cemetery.

Generation IV

Andrew Bear Hackman owned land in Warwick Township, Lancaster County. He was a farmer and served for many years as a justice of the peace. In 1867, he sold land to the Warwick Township School District for the building of a school along the road from Oregon to Lititz.[42] In 1895, he received a merit award from the Ephrata Marble and Granite Works. No one in the family seems to have any recollection of Andrew's carving of marble. His teacher was Samuel Coldren.[43]

On 5 September 1861, Andrew married Martha Eschbach Brenner of Millersville, Lancaster County, Pennsylvania.[44] They were married at B. Kauffman's Tavern by the Reverend Jacob Reinhold.[45] Martha was the daughter of   Jacob Brenner,[46] and Susanna   Eshbach.[47]   Andrew   and   Martha subscribed to the United Zion Children Faith.

---

42 Deed P 13 570, 1867, Recorded 1891, Lancaster County Courthouse, Lancaster, Pennsylvania.

43 Reward of Merit, presented to A.B. Hackman by Samuel Coldren, instructor, mailed 27 April 1895, special delivery, from Ephrata Marble and Granite Works, Geo. Bolster & Sons, Prop's. (Branch Yard at Manheim, Pa. Opposite Washington House.)

44 Family Bible published 1835, held by Henry H. Hackman.

45 News clipping held by Henry H. Hackman. The name of the paper is not included in the clipping.

46 Deed Book N 9 580, 1 April 1863. Deed Book N 12 457, Jacob Brenner will, X 1 493, 11 June 1853, Probated 8 October 1862, Lancaster County Courthouse, Lancaster, Pennsylvania.

For a time Andrew and Martha lived on Main Street, Lititz, Lancaster County, Pennsylvania. After Martha's death, Andrew lived in the home of his son, Willis. On Saturday nights Andrew would stay with his grandchildren while Willis and Anna, his wife, went to the Brunswick in Lancaster to see the vaudeville show. Willis and Anna would have taken the children along for this outing, but the younger ones fell asleep, and Willis, being practical, did not care to purchase tickets for slumbering children.[48]

In his later years, Andrew was very concerned about leaving the graves of his loved ones in good repair and in locations where they would not be forgotten. In 1915, he went to Rapho Township and asked permission of Allen G. Becker to transport the stone of his father, David Hackman, to the Millport Cemetery in Warwick Township. The permission was granted. Andrew left the remains of his father in the private cemetery and placed a new stone over them. He rebuilt the one stone and placed it in the Hackman portion of the Millport Cemetery, consequently, David Hackman has two stones.[49] Andrew rebuilt the stone of his sister, Anna, in the Hammercreek Cemetery. The back of the stone, shown below, says "Rebuilt by A.B. Hackman, bro., 5 July 1913."

Andrew also placed in the Hammercreek Mennonite cemetery, stones in memory of "Grandfather and Grandmother Hackman." (stones are shown on the next page) We do not know if the

47 Mennonite File Drawer, Mennonite Center, Lancaster, Pennsylvania. We have not been able to verify this surname.
48 Henry H. Hackman interview, September, 1976, by Elaine Hackman Grace.
49 Henry H. Hackman and Minnie Becker Hackman both remember this incident. Also the two stones are available in their respective locations for inspection. The back of the Millport stone is inscribed "Rebuilt 1915".

old stones were so worn that he could not read them or if he simply placed stones there as a memorial to his grandparents. It seems odd that he did not include their names unless he did not know them. He was only about three years old when his father died. His mother, Susanna, remarried and

Martha Eschbach (Brenner) Hackman (1839-1913)

died in 1886. Perhaps by the time Andrew was
interested in his family background the information
was "lost." In the picture of the grandmother and
grandfather stones (next page), sister Anna's stone

can be seen in the middle. To the right, but not included in the picture, are the stones of John G. and Susanna Brubaker, the stepfather and mother of Andrew and Anna Hackman.

Andrew and Martha Hackman from a tin type photograph likely taken soon after their marriage in 1861. A touched-up crop of this picture was used for the cover of this book. The original image is in the possession of Lawrence Knorr, a 2nd great grandson..

Quilt by Martha E B Hackman for her son Willis Brenner Hackman. This quilt is in the possession of Lawrence Knorr, a great grandson of Willis.

In the Summer of 1916, there was a row of corn missing in the cornfield on the Hackman farm. People said it was an omen. Surely enough, on 27 July 1916, Andrew B. Hackman passed away. He was buried in Millport Cemetery. He was sorely missed by his grandson, Henry, who now at the tender age of eight, stayed alone with his younger brothers Willis (age 7), Walter (age 5) and Richard (age 3) while his parents and older brother, Andrew, went to see the vaudeville shows on Saturday at the Brunswick.[50]

Andrew B. Hackman and Martha E. Brenner Hackman had issue:[51]

Alice Ann B. Hackman, born 1 January 1862, died 26 June 1894, married John E Leed, born 11

---

50 Henry Hess Hackman interview, September, 1976, by Elaine Hackman Grace.
51 Family Bible published 1835, held by Henry H Hackman.

September 1854, died 13 September 1948. Both are buried in Millport Cemetery.[52]

Emma Amelia Hackman, born 13 February 1868, married John Grube.[53]

Romanus Andrew B. Hackman, born 30 November 1871, died 18 January 1873, buried in Millport Cemetery.

Willis Brenner Hackman, born 21 September 1877, died 11 August 1947, married April 1902[54] to (1) Anna Hess, born 12 October 1879, died 27 August 1917, daughter of Henry L. Hess and Sarah Hess.[55] Married (2) Emma Geib Kreiner, born 5 September 1880, died 6 October 1958. All are buried in the Millport Mennonite Church Cemetery, Warwick Township, Lancaster County, Pennsylvania.

---

52 Information obtained from Henry H. Hackman interview, September, 1976.
53 Ibid.
54 Wedding certificate held by Henry H Hackman.
55 Information obtained from Henry H. Hackman interview, September, 1976.

Generation V

(This very personal account of the life in the home of Willis and Anna Hackman is shared with us by their son, Henry H. Hackman. The incidents are accurate only as they impressed him as a child. Unless otherwise noted, the information was gathered in September 1976 interviews.)

Willis Brenner Hackman was a chicken farmer in Millport, Warwick Township, Lancaster County, Pennsylvania. On 3 April 1902, he married Anna Hess at the residence of Reverend John M Lefever in Neffsville, Lancaster County, Pennsylvania.[56] Anna Hess was the daughter of Henry Landis Hess and Sarah Weidler Hess.

Anna was a large woman, weighing 315 pounds and standing six feet and one-half inch in stocking feet. She held a teacher's provisional certificate,[57] and taught school during the years of 1899, 1900 and 1901. Anna had an aunt, her father's sister Maria, who was deaf and dumb. Maria (1855-1933)[58] had been sent to a school for handicapped children where she learned to talk with her hands. Later, Maria married Timothy Purvis (1863-1949)[59] who was also deaf and dumb. In spite of their

---

56 Wedding certificate held by Henry H Hackman.
57 Provisional certificates numbered 63, 301, 271, signed by M J Brecht, Superintendent. These are in the possession of Henry H Hackman.
58 Gravestone in the Landis Valley Mennonite Church Cemetery, Lancaster County, Pennsylvania.
59 Ibid.

Anna Hess Hackman (1879-1917)

handicaps, they were able to operate their own stand at the Lancaster Farmer's Market and care for their own needs. When Maria came to visit Anna, the two ladies would converse busily with their hands. Anna's young children found this type of conversation amusing and would sit on a bench behind the kitchen table and giggle. This rude behavior offended their mother who severely reprimanded them; however, she was never known to spank or slap her children.

Although Anna was relatively welleducated, she was offended by the state's new ruling in favor of compulsory vaccinations for small pox. Her children had such sore arms. She found it inconceivable that people in Harrisburg would cause little children to suffer so much. She carefully placed plastic shields over the sore areas to protect them, probably causing the vaccinations to heal even more slowly.

When Willis and Anna noticed that Henry, one of their preschool children, was ruptured they took him to Lancaster to be fitted with a truss. A special truss had to be made since Henry was so small. Henry wore the truss periodically, but the rupture did not heal. Finally, Willis took him to a pow-wow doctor. The doctor put something over Henry's eyes so he couldn't see, said a few words, and sent him home. For whatever reason, the rupture healed.

About 1912 or 1913, the first motor car came through the Millport area. The Hackman children thought it was a team of runaway horses. The tickatut, tickatut sound was caused by the vehicles buggy wheels. It had a steering wheel, and not a stick to steer it.

Willis and Anna had a family of boys. Myrtle, the first child and only daughter, had died when she was just two months old. The five boys were rough, tough farm boys and learned how to do a man's job at a very early age. Henry, alone, enjoyed playing with dolls. One evening, his brothers put his dolls in the cook-stove oven. By morning there was nothing left of the dolls but a charred mass of wire and metal washers and a deep, empty ache in a little boy's heart.

The poultry business requires a great deal of investment and skill. Chicks are delicate creatures, easily contracting illnesses, and they must be painstakingly cared for. It was the job of the sons, Henry, Willis, and Walter to clean the chick houses. On one occasion, the boys chased the chicks out of the house into the enclosed yard in order to prepare the house for cleaning. But the chicks huddled together in the corners, some suffocating. Willis was so angry at this irresponsible behavior on the part of his sons that he gave the oldest one, Henry, a solid whack on the back of the neck. The area was infested with ringworm. Henry felt something warm run down his neck. He was sent into the house to his mother, Anna, who tenderly bathed his wound as she tried to hide the tears that kept spilling onto her cheeks.

It was a hard life. The sons in the Hackman family were respected for their physical prowess and their ability to work. Although love was present in the family, there was very little tenderness demonstrated. Willis seemed to consider demonstrative love a weakness, not to be indulged in by "man." Anna showed her love in little ways, especially appreciated by Henry.

When the sons were quite small, they were expected to do the work of men. Henry helped his Grandfather Hess plant tobacco. Grandfather Hess put a footrest on the tobacco planter, because Henry was so young he did not "fit" the planter, which was designed for adult use. After they worked two days, Grandfather Hess asked, "How much do you want for working?"

"Oh, about a dollar," replied little Henry.

"I'll give you two dollars," said Grandfather Hess, "One for working and one because you are my namesake."

Once a week water was heated on the cook stove for baths. It was then poured into wooden tubs, and five little boys got their Saturday night washing.

The Sunnyside School that Willis's oldest son, Andrew, attended was adjoining the Hackman farm. In fact, Grandfather Andrew Hackman had sold the land to the Warwick School District.[60] On his first trip to visit the school, Henry was fascinated by the ink well on his desk. He put his finger in it. The Sunnyside School closed before the second son, Henry, began school. Andrew and Henry together attended the Millport School. In his first year at school, Henry came home to tell his mother, "Mom, what do you think? Tomorrow the teacher is going to give us tables." No amount of explaining by his mother could convince Henry that the teacher was not going to provide tables for the children to play on. Another day at school Henry was asked to recite 'Twinkle Little Star'. He obliged. "Twinkle, twinkle little star, how I wonder how you ever got up there!" All the children laughed, and Henry couldn't understand why.

At the end of Henry's first year of school, the Millport School was closed. Andrew and Henry walked the two miles to Rothsville to attend school. Seven year-old Henry climbed the long imposing front steps (they are still there), and saw an elderly gentleman standing in the hall. Henry asked him, "Where shall I go?"

Joe Moon, the janitor, answered, "I think you should go in there."

60 Andrew B Hackman to Warwick Township School District Deed P 13 570, 9 August 1867, recorded 20 February 1891, Lancaster County Courthouse, Lancaster, Pennsylvania.

Finding no better alternative, Henry entered. School was easy that year as he inadvertently repeated first grade.

The first airplane flew over Millport in about 1916 while Willis and his sons, Andrew, Henry, Willis and Walter (Richard was too small) were succoring tobacco in the field. When Willis heard the plane, he sent Henry into the house to call Anna. Henry thought it was the sound of a motorcycle. What an experience to look up and see that mechanical bird flying through the air!

About 1916, Willis purchased a Peerless. He took his family on an excursion to Gettysburg. When the family arrived at Gettysburg, Willis was so busy looking around that he banged into another vehicle. The Peerless lay on its side in the lane of oncoming traffic. Anna, who was pregnant, received an injury to her shin.

This was an extremely difficult time for Anna. The wound became infected and refused to heal. Her great weight coupled with the injured shin (now a gaping hole of about an inch in diameter and extending to the bone) caused her a great deal of pain in her leg and feet. Henry often rubbed his mother's feet for her. Anna's pregnancy terminated in an abnormally large child. It was born dead or died immediately after birth. It's grave in the Millport Church Cemetery is simply marked "Baby."

There was a row of corn missing again in the Hackman farm in 1917. This time the omen was for Anna. On the evening of 27 August 1917, Willis called to his oldest son, Andrew. "Go down to Zook's mill and call the doctor. Maybe Mom's dead."

Anna was gone, and the family prepared for her funeral. Willis took his five young sons to Groff and Wolf in Lancaster and bought each one a new suit of clothes. At the store, he wept. Years later, when Henry, as an adult, returned to the store to purchase a suit, the clerk was to remember the gentleman who had brought five young sons into the store to buy suits for their mother's funeral. He asked Henry if he had been one of the boys. Indeed he had been.

It was a busy time. The farm and house had to be tidied and made ready for the funeral. Many people came to pay their respects. Anna's brother, Elmer Hess, arrived from Illinois. There was so much activity around the farm. There was little time to feel the loss.

The day of the funeral was stifling hot. The Millport Community Church (now the Millport Mennonite Church) was crowded, and there was not a breath of moving air. After the funeral, dinner was served in the Hackman tobacco shed.

The impact of Anna's passing fell with a crushing blow as the guests and "larger family" departed. Son Henry, now nine, attempted to complete his daily chores, taking care of the chickens. He sobbed in utter despair as he stumbled to the chicken house, took care of the chickens, and returned to the house. Anna had always kept clean clothes neatly folded in drawers ready for her children when they needed them. Henry pulled open his drawer to get his clean clothes and found the drawer empty. Feeling complete abandonment, he once again wept for the lost link of comfort and tenderness.

Willis had a large farm to run. He could not be expected to play the roles of father and mother. Son Andrew, now fourteen, was needed to help with the farm work. That left Henry, now nine, to help as best he could around the house. Henry cooked – mostly meat pudding and potatoes. He washed the dishes with homemade soap and wished his Mom were there to help get the dishes clean. The grease simply would not wash away.

Before too long, Minnie Shall (or Shawl) came to wash and clean, and on 30 March 1918, Willis married his second wife, Emma Geib Kreiner. She was a widow with four children: Henry, Herman, Ivan and Florence. Florence, alone, came along to live with her mother in the Hackman family. Willis had courted Emma before he married Anna.

Emma wasted no time. She got the house back in order and got busy in the garden. She was an excellent cook, and by the end of the summer, she had enough vegetables to make her delicious chow-chow. When she had the chow-chow prepared and ready for canning, she called Henry to empty the scraps. He came, picked up the buckets and dumped their contents in the chicken house for the chickens. Minutes later when Emma was ready to put her chow-chow into cans, she found only the scraps. Henry had dumped the chow-chow in the chicken house.

The children in Willis Hackman's family, like all other children in all other generations, were exposed to good and not-so-good teachers. Times really do not change all that much. One teacher of outstanding quality was Miss Lillian Becker, later Mrs. Lillian Eberly. Miss Becker taught the ninth grade in the basement of the Rothsville School. There was no bell in the basement to signal the end of classes. Miss Becker solved that problem by using a little alarm clock, Henry thought it would be great fun to reset the alarm. At noontime he quietly changed the alarm so that it would ring in the middle of the class period. Surely enough, the clock rang. Miss Becker was not noticeably disturbed. She turned off the alarm without so much as a wince and continued the class. This was too much for Henry. He reset the alarm on several more occasions. It seemed impossible to disturb Miss Becker. She never said a word, only walked over, turned off the alarm, and continued the class. This was no fun. Henry decided to make the incident more interesting. He took a string and tied the alarm switch to the clock leg so that the alarm could not be so easily turned off. Again the alarm rang in the midst of class. Miss Becker, again, walked over, tore the string, turned off the alarm, and continued the class. The challenge was too much for Henry. Not to be outdone, he wrapped and wrapped the string around the alarm switch and securely fastened it. How would Miss Becker handle this one? In the middle of class the alarm rang. As was by now her custom, Miss Becker walked over to turn it off. Alas, the string was too tight. Although she tried, there was no budging the string. Slowly the red color crept into Miss Becker's face. The alarm continued to ring until it was completely unwound. With perfect composure, only the telltale red betraying her, Miss Becker paused long enough for the alarm to deplete itself, and continued the class. At dismissal time, she excused the children one by one with an individual question. "Do you know anything about the alarm?" Each time the response was "no," and the child were dismissed. Twenty-nine times Miss Becker asked the same question. "Do you know anything about the alarm?" Twenty-nine times the answer was "no." And Henry sat and listened. Miss Becker was getting closer and closer. It was a mighty uncomfortable feeling. Finally, there was only one child left – Henry. Miss Becker had saved him for last, and he had been caught in her trap.

Soon after that incident Emma said to her stepson, "Henry, ask Miss Becker to come for dinner." Wow! Were they going to punish him? How much did they know? Henry asked Miss Becker for dinner. He never knew whether there was an ulterior motive in the invitation.

Willis was a strict disciplinarian. His authority was never questioned by his sons. Although they were strong, rugged individuals, they lived by the law of their father. Henry and his brothers worked the chicken houses on the hill. The houses were small. In one of the houses Henry kept his rabbits. One winter when there was ice over the field, and Henry should have been tending the chickens, he stopped to see his rabbits. Suddenly he heard his father approaching. Quickly he ran across the icy field. Willis attempted to follow and give his son a good boot in the seat of the pants. Adults are not as agile on the ice as their offspring. When he tried to place his good, hard kick Willis lost his balance and fell with a thud on the hard ice. Henry was not accustomed to being the victor in a confrontation with his father. He found this experience satisfying.

In a period of three years, two daughters were born to Willis and Emma. Violet Gertrude and Emma Amelia added a touch of femininity to this formerly all-male family.

As he approached his teen years, Henry never thought of his father as having an interest in the aesthetic. He thought Willis in strictly pragmatic terms – getting work done in the most efficient manner, investing money wisely, respecting strength and skill. One day, driving to the farm from Rothsville, Henry sat beside his father in the Hudson sedan. He was tremendously impressed when Willis said, "Isn't that a beautiful sunset?" It was the first time he had heard Willis express an appreciation for the aesthetic wonders of nature.

Once a year Willis gave his sons money. It was Millport Fair time. At the picnic grounds, people gathered to hear the band, visit together, buy pop, and, in general, have a good time. Henry, Willis and Walter (Andrew was too grown up and Richard was too small) each received a dime. There was no allowance during the year, but the boys could spend this ten cents any way they wished. At the band concert portion of the fair, an offering was taken to help defray the expenses incurred. Henry felt responsibility to contribute his share, so when the plate passed him, he dropped in one of his two nickels.

When Henry was ready to enter high school, the educational system played another trick on him. Elementary school had consisted of grades one through nine. High school should have consisted of grades ten through twelve. Now Rothsville was about to initiate a four year high school program. Although henry had completed ninth grade on the elementary level, he was now obliged to attend ninth grade on the high school level.

The Hackman sons learned to work, and work, and work! Work, well done with speed and accuracy, was a source of great pride for Willis. He was extremely proud of the working capabilities of his sons. He carefully taught them how to conserve their energies while accomplishing unbelievable quantities of work. He insisted that, when they hoed tobacco on the hill, they always walk on the lower side of the row. By doing this, they would reverse the hoe at the end of each row, and a different set of muscles was used. Thus, every other row was hoed in a right-handed manner, and every other row was hoed in a left-handed manner. The person doing the hoeing did not get so tired.

The neighbors were well aware of the working talents of the Hackman boys. Walter, Willis and Henry were in demand at threshing time. The three of them worked the mow, throwing the sheaves of wheat to the threshing machine. Again, Willis's teaching was evidenced. The boys rotated their positions and reversed their throwing direction periodically in order to keep fresh. "Get the

Hackman boys if you can," was the advice of the owners of the threshing rig.

A tremendous mutual respect developed between father and sons. Willis was proud to have his sons in such demand. The sons looked with equal respect upon the father who had taught them how to be successful. They were allowed to keep for themselves the money they earned working for the neighbors.

In the winter, the country roads had to be shoveled. There were no snowplows, and the snow came just the same. The neighborhood men got together to shovel the drifts of snow. All the men were bundled up with warm coats, gloves, scarves, and caps. Even with their warm gloves their hands were cold. That is, all but the Hackman men. They worked along with the rest of the neighbors, but Willis and his sons needed no gloves. They were Hackman stock!

A family of five boys could hardly be expected to survive the adolescent stage without at least one serious accident. One Sunday evening when he was about fifteen, Henry was riding a neighbor's bicycle. When he reached Zook's Mill, he was hit by a car. The driver stopped the car. Not sure what had happened, he backed up to see if he had hit anything. By doing this, he drove over Henry two times. Henry had severe internal injuries and a broken arm.

Henry had been an excellent underwater swimmer. His superb physical condition gave him unusual lung capacity. Now, as he lay in his hospital bed with intense chest pains, he pretended he was swimming under water. He breathed as little as possible and carefully regulated every breath of air entering and leaving his chest cavity. He made a promise to join the church if he survived this ordeal.

*Willis and Emma Hackman at the Millport farm,
shortly before Willis died.*

At first, Dr. Atlee, Sr. of Lancaster, thought it would be necessary to amputate Henry's left hand. It was terribly mangled, but upon closer examination, he discovered that there were no bones broken. So he carefully stitched the hand as best he could. Four years later a piece of glass thrust its way through the skin.

When Henry was well enough to leave the hospital, Dr. Atlee said, "When you came in here, I didn't expect you to leave through the front door."

At home, Henry found all the junk cleaned up around the farm. "When did you have time to do all of this?" he asked his father.

With emotion in his voice, his father replied, "We were getting ready for your funeral."

About this time Willis wondered where his oldest son, Andrew, spent his Saturday nights. He suggested that Henry secretly get in the trunk of Andrew's car and ride along. Andrew had a Buick Roadster. He could put the top down. In the trunk there was an oval hole big enough for Henry to lie in. Henry took the key to see if he could lock the truck from the inside. Then he took a stick and placed it so that it would not be possible to open the trunk from the outside. The plan worked. He waited for Saturday to arrive.

On the next page: Pictures of the Willis Hackman farm at Millport taken in the summer of 1976. The house was in the process of being remodeled and landscaped. The barn has since been partially demolished. During his lifetime, Willis always kept his farm buildings in excellent repair.

Late the following Saturday afternoon Andrew was planning to go to the Hopeland picnic. Henry quickly milked the cows and crawled into the trunk of the car. He waited about fifteen minutes. Andrew came, and off they went. Andrew drove terribly fast. (Henry later discovered that he was trying to race someone to the crossing.) The car bumped and swerved. Henry decided this was too much for him. He opened the trunk a peep to see if he could jump out. There was no possible escape. Thank goodness, in a short time Andrew slowed down, and Henry's ride was a bit more comfortable.

This sense of security was not to last. The car soon stopped. Andrew only needed gas, and in no time they were on their way again. Before long the car stopped again – a flat tire! Andrew went to the trunk to get the jack. He tried to open the trunk but found that he didn't have his key. He found a screwdriver and tried to pry the trunk open. It would not budge. Finally, in disgust, he gave up, walked to a neighbor's farm, and borrowed tools to change the tire. Once again they were off.

When they arrived at the picnic grounds, Andrew parked the car and walked off. Henry stayed in the trunk for awhile, but finally the music was too much for him, and he stealthily lifted the lid to look around. This was risky. He settled back in his oval space and lowered the lid. In the darkness he saw the lid move. A hand reached in and felt around. Henry whispered, "Put the lid down. I want to see where my brother goes." He had no idea to whom the hand belonged.

When Andrew returned to the car, he had with him two girls and a boy. The Buick Roadster had one seat. The four of them crowded into the roadster. Andrew did not drive very fast. They went down the road, turned right at a sandstone mill and later turned left. Finally, they stopped, and one couple got out and went to the house. Andrew and his girl stayed in the car. She teased him to tell her his age. She guessed he was about twenty-two. Actually, he was not that old. Henry thoroughly enjoyed his eavesdropping.

Completely unaware that they had company in the trunk, Andrew and his young lady friend completed their visit in the car and went into the house. Henry opened the trunk and looked around. He made mental notes of the farm. It was not in too good repair, and the barn was built in a style he thought his father would recognize. The two girls stayed at the farm. Andrew drove the other boy home.

It was a beautiful moonlit night. On the way home Andrew drove slowly, and Henry once again opened the trunk. He sat on the deck with the lid on his lap enjoying the beautiful night when he suddenly noticed that the moon was casting his shadow on the bank immediately to the drivers left. He was afraid to move lest Andrew should notice. He sat quite still until they came to their own farm, and Andrew drove slowly around the barn. Henry quickly jumped off, washed his feet at the pump, and fled to the security of his bed.

There were three beds in the room. Andrew slept in one of them. Willis and Henry shared the second bed. Walter and Richard slept in the third one. As he crept into bed and pulled up the covers, Henry remembered the wet footprints that he had left around the pump and on the walk to the house. Would Andrew see them? Andrew entered the room. Henry groaned as if he had been in bed for a long time. "What's wrong Henry?" asked Andrew. He apparently had not seen the wet footprints. Henry obviously did not answer.

The next day was Sunday. There was a great deal of company at the Hackman home. Willis had told his visiting step-sons about Henry's adventures the night before. They asked Andrew, "Did you know Henry was in the back of the car last night?"

"Yes, Henry, tell us about last night," encouraged Willis.

Henry loved the special attention. He recounted the events of the night before much to his father's delight and his brother's embarrassment and anger.

As a sixteen year-old, Henry was interested in electricity. With the help of his brothers, he engineered a dam in the meadow on his father's farm. The dam was carefully constructed so as to utilize the water power to furnish electricity. The Rothsville School Library did not include the books Henry needed to use to find the answers to his questions about electricity so he went to the Lancaster City Library. Here he found the necessary reading materials. He applied and adapted the knowledge he found in the books to his own set of circumstances and homemade equipment. Willis purchased for the boys the few pieces of junkyard materials that they needed for their project. For a whole summer the boys spent Sunday afternoons and any other precious spare moments working on the dam. By the end of the summer, they had constructed a dam which could produce power to run a 32 volt generator. "Perhaps," thought Henry, "I can harness enough water power to make electricity for the whole farm."

All through high school Henry played basketball, his first love. He started playing varsity basketball when he was in elementary ninth grade. By the time he was a senior, he and many of his teammates were disqualified for high school competition, because they were playing varsity ball for five consecutive years. They played the regular schedule on a disqualified basis. Rothsville was an extremely small school. The basketball team played teams representing schools several times their size. Henry played guard. When Rothsville played Quarryville for the championship, Henry played opposite the Quarryville forward, Oatman. Oatman was averaging 23 points a game, a really high average for that time. The morning following the game, the paper had this sports headline: 'Hackman Holds Oatman Scoreless.' Willis was extremely pleased, as he was of all his sons when they excelled in the physical arena. Despite his pride, he never saw Henry play basketball in high school or later in college where Henry enjoyed equal success on the basketball court.

It was the custom of Willis to present a beautiful gold watch to each son who reached his seventeenth birthday without smoking. Of course, the admonition, "If I ever catch you smoking, I'll give you the damndest licking you ever got!," was equally strong motivation to refrain from smoking. Willis seemed to know intuitively that smoking was not good for one's physical well-being.

Henry graduated from Rothsville High School. At that time, it was the exception, rather than the rule for farm children to complete high school. There was usually too much work on the family farm to allow a child the luxury of sitting in a high school classroom. Then, too, there was always the transportation problem for farm children. Despite the abundance of work on his farm, Willis permitted Henry to attend high school. Upon Henry's graduation, Willis presented him with a $50 gold piece, a symbol of his pride in Henry's accomplishment. Henry was deeply moved. His father was not noted for giving gifts. Henry treasured the gold piece for a great deal more than its substantial monetary worth. The gold piece was invaluable simply because it was a gift from his father. No amount of money could have bought the joy Henry experienced at receiving a gift from his father. It was difficult, years later, to find that illusion shattered. The value of the $50 gold piece was deducted, at Willis's direction, from Henry's share in Willis's estate. The money did not matter. It was the loss of the gift that hurt. Deductions were also required for any gifts made to his other children.

About 1942, Willis and Emma moved from the Millport farm to 23 South Cedar Street, Lititz, Lancaster County, Pennsylvania. Son Richard and his family moved to the Millport farm. The Cedar Street house was directly across the street from the Lititz Elementary and Senior High School. Henry was now living on the Rapho Township farm and teaching science in the Lititz High School. From time to time, he would stop briefly to see his father and step-mother. Working two jobs left little time for lengthy visits. One day, he took along a homemade bologna. It had come from one of his farm animals, and he wished to share it with his father.

"How much do I owe you, Henry?" Willis asked.

"Nothing," replied Henry, "It's just a very small token of appreciation for the many things you have done for me."

Willis was choked with emotion. "Well, thank you, Henry," he finally managed to say.

In excellent health, Willis continued to work on the chicken farm even after he had moved to town. At seventy, he was strong and agile, able to compete physically with men much younger than he. Unfortunately, it was a small cut on his forehead 'too small to bother about,' which caused his untimely death. In August 1947, the Lititz newspaper carried this article:

LOCK-JAW CAUSES DEATH W. HACKMAN
Scratch of Forehead Thought Source of Infection: Funeral Today.

Lock-jaw which developed from a scratch caused the sudden death this week of Willis B. Hackman, of 23 South Cedar Street, this borough, who died Monday at 12:35 PM at the Lancaster General Hospital.

According to friends, Hackman sustained the scratch on his forehead while working at his chicken house last Friday. It was thought he scratched the skin open with a piece of chicken-wire, but he informed friends later that he had pricked the skin open with the end of a pick.

Wiping the blood away with his hand, he continued working for some time without applying any medication to the slight wound. On Saturday morning, Mr. Hackman attended his business in the center of the borough.

At that time his jaw was drawn slightly to one side and he complained that it was becoming more painful. Friends advised him to go to a physician immediately.

After examining him, Dr. Franklin K Cassel, South Broad Street, ordered Mr. Hackman removed immediately to the Lancaster General Hospital. His condition continued to draw steadily worse until his death.

He was seventy years of age and lived in this borough for the past five years when he moved here from his farm at Millport. He was a member of the Church of the Brethren here.

Besides his wife, Emma Geib Hackman, he is survived by these children: Andrew and Henry Hackman, both of Manheim R 2, Willis Hackman, Millway, Walter Hackman, Ephrata, Richard Hackman, Millport, Violet, wife of Dr. Roy Pfaltzgraff, both medical missionaries at Nigeria, Africa; and Emma, wife of W W White, Highspire; four step children: Herman Kreiner, Elizabethtown, Henry F and Ivan Kreiner, both of Manheim R 2, and Florence, wife of William Frey, Lititz R 4. Thirty grandchildren, four great-grandchildren and a sister, Mrs. Emma Grube, Neffsville, also survives.

Services will be held this afternoon at 1:30 from Beck Brothers Funeral Home followed by further services in the Church of the Brethren. Internment will be made in the Millport Cemetery.

After the death of Willis, Emma married Reuben Myer. They lived at Brickerville, Lancaster County, Pennsylvania. Emma died 6 October 1958.[61] Although she was widowed three times and had three husbands, Emma asked to be buried with her second husband, Willis Brenner Hackman.

Willis Brenner Hackman and Anna Hess Hackman had issue:

Myrtle Hackman, born 11 December 1902, died 11 February 1903, buried at Disston Meeting House, which is now Millport Mennonite Church Cemetery.[62]

Andrew Hess Hackman, born 17 December 1903, died 29 June 1964, buried at Hernley's Mennonite Church Cemetery, Lancaster County, Pennsylvania, married Ada Horst, born 16 November 1903, died 1 January 1978, daughter of Jonas N. Horst (22 November 1874 – 25 May 1963) and Ada Stone Hackman (25 August 1875 – 18 November 1930). Andrew and Ada were married 1 January 1925 at New Holland by Bishop Noah Marks. Andrew was a farmer with land adjoining

---

61 Death Remembrance, Beck Brothers Funeral Directors. Held by Henry H Hackman.

62 Family Bible, presented to Willis B Hackman from Andrew B Hackman, on 1 April 1902. Held by Henry H Hackman.

Manheim Borough, Lancaster County, Pennsylvania. No issue.[63]

Henry Hess Hackman, born 27 July 1908, died 24 September 1987, married Minnie Mae Becker, born 1 May 1913, died 6 May 1982, daughter of Reverend Allen Grabill Becker (11 October 1873 – 28 August 1951) and Lizzie Witmer Heisey (18 March 1888 – 7 September 1954), of Rapho Township, Lancaster County, Pennsylvania. Henry and Minnie were married 28 May 1933, in the Lititz Church of the Brethren by Dr. A. C. Baugher.[64] Married 16 July 1983, Elizabethtown Church of the Brethren, Mildred Burkholder McDonnel.

Willis Hess Hackman, born 21 November 1909, died 20 August 1989, married Mary Ebersole Martin, New Holland, Lancaster County, Pennsylvania, born 6 February 1914, died 22 March 1999, daughter of Amos M. Martin (7 July 1884 – 17 march 1958) and Minnie E. Ebersole (8 July 1886 – 18 December 1926). Willis and Mary were married 19 December 1931.[65]

Walter Hess Hackman, born 7 April 1911, died 29 December 2002, married Margaret Bucher Boose of West Cocalico Township, Lancaster County, Pennsylvania, born 1 October 1917, died 28 December 2002, daughter of Harry Boose (27 September 1876 – 20 June 1936) and Susanna Bucher (6 September 1877 – 9 May 1963). Walter and Margaret were married 6 April 1935.[66]

---

63 Letter received in 1976 from Ada Hackman, Landis Homes Retirement Community, RD 3, Lititz, Pennsylvania. Held by Elaine Hackman Grace.

64 Minnie Mae Hackman interview, September 1976, RD 2, Manheim, Lancaster County, Pennsylvania.

65 Mary Hackman letter, 1976, RD 3 Elizabethtown, Lancaster County, Pennsylvania. Held by Elaine Hackman Grace.

66 Margaret Hackman letter, 1976, 144 East Walnut Street, Ephrata, Lancaster County, Pennsylvania. Held by Elaine

Richard Hess Hackman, born 25 August 1913, died 26 March 1996, married Betty Forney, born 23 April 1909, died 29 November 1989, daughter of John Kreider Forney (20 March 1882 – 22 March 1969) and Clara Baker Yost (1886 – 1920). Richard and Betty were married 25 August 1934.[67] He subsequently married Mary Dubble on 19 August 1990.[68]

Baby Hackman, died at birth (circa 1915) and buried at Millport Cemetery. Anna died soon after the death of this child.[69]

Willis Brenner Hackman and Emma Geib Hackman had issue:

Violet Gertrude Hackman, born 7 July 1919, married Roy Pfaltzgraff, MD, son of George Nevin Pfalztgraff, York, York County, Pennsylvania, and Mary Roth of Mennonite background.[70]

Emma Amelia Hackman, born 28 May 1921, died 3 November 1994, married William W. White, born 31 May 1923, died 31 August 1998, the son of William Walter White and Catherine (Wolf) White of Highspire, on 7 August 1942 at St. Peter's Lutheran Church in Highspire, Pennsylvania.[71]

Hackman Grace.
67 Betty Hackman letter, 1976, RD 3, Lititz, Lancaster County, Pennsylvania held by Elaine Hackman Grace.
68 Elaine Hackman Grace letter, 1994, held by Lawrence Knorr.
69 Ibid.
70 Violet Pfaltzgraff letter, 1976, Garkida, via Yola, Gongola, Nigeria, held by Elaine Hackman Grace.
71 Knorr, Lawrence, *The Relations of Milton Snavely Hershey, 4th Ed,* (Sunbury Press, New Kingstown, PA 2007), page 163.

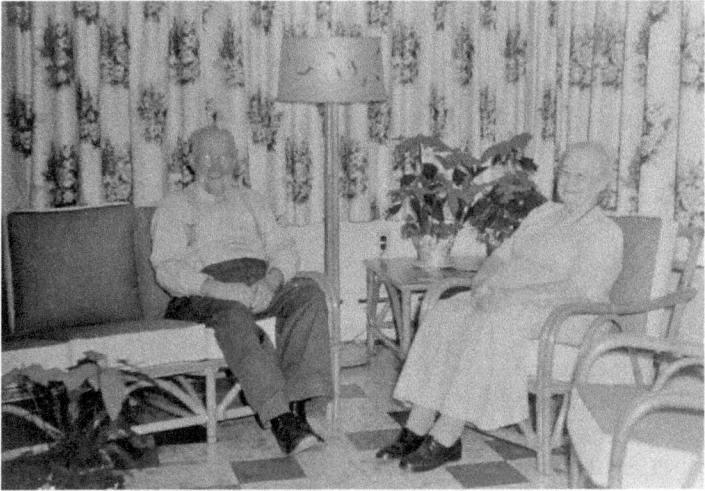

Emma Geib Hackman Myer with her third husband, Reuben Myer circa 1956 at their retirement home.

Generation VI

Henry Hess Hackman left his Millport home to attend college at Elizabethtown, Lancaster County, Pennsylvania. He took the trolley from Lititz to Elizabethtown. At the end of College Avenue in Elizabethtown, he got off the trolley and walked to the college. He attended summer school and worked part time helping to build the new gym.

During his second year of summer school, Henry decided to take a brief break and go home. He took the trolley from Elizabethtown to Lititz. It was a hot day. He knew that his father and brothers would be busy in the fields, so he carried his two big suitcases full of laundry (there were no automatic washers and dryers at the college) and walked the four miles to the farm at Millport. He planned to surprise his family. Hot, tired, and thirsty, he reached the farmhouse door. His stepmother looked up and saw him.

"What do you want here? We didn't know you were coming!" she asked.

Henry walked up the steps in tears. He had walked four hard, tiring miles to surprise his family, only to discover he wasn't wanted.

Henry experienced a lonely, rejected feeling for the next year or two. He tried to re-evaluate family ties and friendships. He kept hearing rumors of his father's sometimes unkind treatment of his mother, Anna. In his desire to discover the truth and hopefully prove rumors false, he sought the council of his mother's brother-in-law, Abram Huber. Uncle

Abram was married to Anna's sister, Bessie. Surely, his mother would have confided in Aunt Bessie, and Uncle Abram would know if anything had been wrong. When Henry confronted Uncle Abram with his question, he received this reply:

"Well, Henry, I can only say this. I wish my boys would have as much respect for me as your father's boys have for him."

Sometime later, when he had met Minnie Becker, Henry went to the Millport farm on a Saturday evening. No one was home. He took all his things and moved them to the Becker's attic. He sent graduation invitations to his family and was disappointed when they did not come to the baccalaureate service. Minnie's parents, Allen and Lizzie Becker were there. "Oh well," thought Henry, "Baccalaureate isn't so important anyway. They will probably be here tomorrow for commencement."

Commencement arrived. The Beckers attended, but Henry's family did not.[72]

Minnie Becker Hackman remembers those college and early married years in such a beautiful and charming way. She refers to Henry Hess Hackman, her husband, as Daddy; her father, Allen Grabill Becker, as Grandpa; her mother, Lizzie Heisey Becker as Grandma. Her account follows verbatim:

Daddy noticed me Saturday morning at a service in the gym at Elizabethtown College which closed a week of what we called 'Young People's Conference' held at the end of the summer term on the college campus. This was the fore-runner of the camp program of the church. I was attending the conference, but Daddy was finishing his summer college work because he was sick during the

72 Henry H Hackman interview, 1976. The first four paragraphs are taken from this interview. Notes of interview held by Elaine Hackman Grace.

summer. I had just finished high school, and as I remember, the other young people were about that age also. This 'about to be college senior' who ate with us in the college dining room and clowned around with us at meal time seemed quite a long way above us – both in age and education. I remembered laughing and laughing at his antics. Therefore, I was really taken by surprise when he asked me to go with him to a party that same Saturday evening. I couldn't go, but he was so persistent that I finally said I could go with him Thursday evening of the following week. I was really quite in awe of the 'college boy' and I didn't want to go. But being very inexperienced, I did not know how to get rid of him. After lunch when Grandma came to take me home, I pointed Daddy out to her. We were all waiting for our parents in front of Alpha Hall, and Daddy was there, too. When Grandma saw him, she said, "That fellow there in the white pants? You don't want to go out with him!" Daddy had an unpopular beginning, but a strong popular acceptance later. on.

At the time, young people in college couldn't afford to have cars, or if they did, they were rather old ones. Daddy's was extremely old, but, if we only had it now, it would be a great antique! It was a Model T Ford two seater. Somewhere along the way, it had lost its top. Also, the door at the driver's seat did not open, and I remember Daddy putting one leg over and then the other when he got into his car.

On our first date, Daddy stopped at the Snavely Farm at East Fairview Church to ask directions. He realized the gas line had a leak, so when he arrived at our home, he had to lift the seat off the car and turn off the gas. Even so, he had lost so much gas that I offered to give him some from Grandma's storage tank. Daddy was so impressed that I gave him gasoline.

Daddy used to work at the college when he was a student. He helped to build the first gym. He worked so well that Elder Gibble, President of the Board of Trustees and supervisor of the work, told the college treasurer, J Z Herr, to pay Daddy five cents an hour more than the other workers because he worked so well. This was during his first summer at the college.

Another work story Daddy remembers quite vividly occurred during his sophomore year. He used to work for a farmer, Mr. Eshelman, near Elizabethtown. (Mr. Eshelman's son, Paul, is or was, industrial arts instructor at Millersville. He was in school at Elizabethtown with Daddy.) One Saturday Daddy was working very hard – ten hours at thirty cents per hour. That evening he double dated with Dr. Frank Cassel's brother, 'Bud'. They took their girls to a show. Because Bud's car was a little better than Daddy's they went in his car. Daddy thought that he out to pay for the tickets. They asked the girls where they wanted to sit, and they chose the most expensive seats – seventy-five cents. That took all of Daddy's pay for the day. Sitting in those comfortable seats, Daddy fell asleep. He was so tired he slept through the entire show and didn't see any of it. It was a most impressive lesson on how hard one had to work for money, and easily it could slip away with nothing to show for it.

Daddy's college was financed with $1,000 which his father gave to each of the boys and also some money, about $1,000, which he inherited from his mother. He really wanted to be an electrical engineer and had planned to go to Millersville. He was a very good basketball player, and the Millersville basketball coach thought he had enlisted him for Millersville. The coach then left to spend the summer at the shore. Daddy wanted to go to summer school and Superintendent of Lancaster County School's, A

Henry Hess Hackman and Minnie Becker Hackman probably taken sometime during the early 1930's.

P Mylin, recommended he go to Elizabethtown because his mother was a member of the Church of the Brethren! (A good reason!)

When he came to Elizabethtown to register (for $10) the management there welcomed him warmly because they would complete their gym that summer and looked forward to playing their first inter-collegiate basketball in the coming year. Daddy did not like chemistry and did not want to take any chemistry courses. J Z Herr, when he registered, said he didn't need to take chemistry, but Dr. A C Baugher persuaded him to try a course with the *promise he could drop it if he disliked it greatly. Daddy gives Dr. Baugher the credit for teaching him to like chemistry and causing him to become a chemistry teacher. He was Dr. Baugher's student assistant in the laboratory for, I believe, at least two years. Later, when Dr. Baugher became president of the college, he invited Daddy to become instructor of chemistry at the college.*

When Elizabethtown played Millersville in basketball in Daddy's first year, Elizabethtown beat Millersville. Daddy played guard and held their star player (a boy from Ephrata against whom he had also played in high school) to only a few points. The Millersville coach, realizing that he had lost a good prospective player, tried to persuade Daddy to come to Millersville the next semester. There was an offer of a scholarship, and since it was also a state college, there would have been a great saving of money. By this time, however, Daddy had already established some college and team loyalties, and perhaps felt that he had been a bit ignored during the summer, so he refused the offer and stayed at Elizabethtown. How glad I am!

When I came to college, Daddy was a senior. At that time, it was quite something for a big popular senior boy to date a little 'no count' freshman girl. It was then that Miss Rebecca Shaeffer, Dean of Women, called me into her office to warn me that 'sometimes big senior boys just play around with little freshman girls.' She really likes Daddy, for she was not exactly a 'goody-goody' herself. I think she felt that I was inadequate to cope with the situation. She had a great influence on all of us. For the most part, we and our fellow students were first generation college students., and we were very 'green' when we arrived on campus. We needed to 'grow up' and have the rough edges knocked off, and grow into gentlemen and ladies. One of the rules for the girls was a lady does not shout to someone on campus from the window of her room. To this day, if someone comes to the house, and I am upstairs and cannot come down, I can hardly bring myself to call from our upstairs window.

One of the requirements for the gentlemen was to wear a jacket to the dining room. One hot day, Daddy went to Miss Schaeffer to protest. "The girls come to eat with low-cut sleeveless dresses. We fellows must wear seven or eight layers of cloth around our necks."

"Mr. Hackman," said Miss Schaeffer, "You don't know how many uncomfortable clothes the girls are wearing under those cool looking dresses."

Miss Schaeffer never got the 'wearing of the jacket' lesson across to Daddy. Years later, while attending Brown University in the summer, the head waiter was to remind him, "Please wear a jacket the next time you come to make up Rotary."

Another incident remembered by Daddy's fellow students took place in Alpha Hall. At that time, the dining room was in the basement, the social room on the first floor, the girls dorm on the second and third floors. A hall ran length-wise through the center of the building. At either end of this hall was a stairway. In the social room Daddy dared a friend to run up one stairway, through the girls dorm upstairs, and down the opposite stairway. He, Daddy, would do the same, starting on the opposite side. After being egged on by the other students, the boy agreed to do it. They both went to their respective stairs. The other boy carried out the plan successfully. Daddy, however, ran up the stair half way, turned, came down, and ran up the opposite stairway coming down again at the same time as the other boy.

"I didn't see you up there," the boy said. "You didn't go up!"

"Oh, yes," said Daddy, "It was too dark and there were too many girls around. That is why you didn't see me when I passed you."

His friend was satisfied, but someone was the tattletale. When he realized the joke that had been played on him, the boy was very angry. So, in order to protect his credibility, Daddy said he would really carry out his end of the bargain. Up he went. He wasn't as lucky as his friend, and whom should he meet as he ran through the girls dorm, but the house mother, Mrs. McCann. Of course, he had to take the reprimanding.

Graduation year, 1931, was still a Depression year. Jobs were hard to get. It was the Fourth of July that Daddy got his teaching job in Newville, Cumberland County, Pennsylvania. During the Depression Grandpa had lost a lot of money through investments that failed. To help to economize we had the telephone taken out. On his way from Newville that night, Daddy stopped at our home to tell me that he had a job. There had been sixty-five applicants. It was quite late, perhaps midnight, and we were all in bed. He didn't wake us, but he left a lovely bouquet of wild roses and honeysuckle, which he had stopped by the wayside to gather, at the door. It was the sweetest bouquet I ever received, and honeysuckle has always been a very 'happy flower' for both of us.

The old Model T Ford was approaching the end of its life, and with some of his early earnings, Daddy bought a pretty little dark blue Plymouth sedan with yellow wheels. One thing I remember that he liked so well about its appearance was the tiny gold pin line that went all around the middle. It was a very good car, and served us do well that Daddy could never feel that any car was as good as a Chrysler product until the Germans conquered him with the Volkswagon.

A group of more aggressive fellows on the campus had a rather exclusive club they called the 'Candles.' Their insignia was a small candle they wore on watch chains which were worn at the time. Of course, if they became engaged, they gave their fiancee the candle to wear. At Christmas, my sophomore year, Daddy gave me his candle. Grandma understood what it meant, but when I said very coyly to Grandpa, "Papa, may I wear this necklace?"

He said rather sternly,"You don't want to wear that!"

Daddy felt so bad, but Grandma, like Mothers do, privately explained to Grandpa, and while he could not approve of my wearing the necklace, he did approve of its meaning. Daddy was happy. He was very fond of Grandpa and Grandma, and Grandpa grew to think that Daddy always did everything right.

Because Daddy had a high regard for Dr. Baugher, he wanted him to perform our wedding ceremony. A C Baugher was moderator of the Lititz Church of the Brethren which was very new. It was the prettiest Brethren Church in the area. He suggested that we be married in that church. I think we were just about the first couple in our immediate area to be married in a Brethren Church. We had no pattern to follow. Dr. Baugher thought it would be a beautiful ceremony to be married at the close of the Sunday morning service. Our invited guests, plus the Lititz congregation, plus the curious who decided to attend the Lititz church that morning, packed the church. We had a 'big wedding'. How we wouldn't want it to be that way, but it was thrilling then. Even Dr. Baugher was excited. He said, "Do you, Minnie Mae Hackman," etc. Miss Martha Martin was bothered by this error. She had fears that we weren't married properly. We had a lovely honeymoon, going to Natural Bridge, Virginia. Daddy lost his expensive hat, and we drove south instead of north when we started home, but otherwise, it was a lovely trip.

I was lucky to be the first one in my class to get a teaching job. In January, I was promised a school in Rapho Township. The Fairview School near the Mt. Hope Nursing Home which is now remodeled into a house, was my first school. Together Daddy and I saved enough money to buy the furniture we needed, and we moved to Newville at the end of the summer, 1933. Because of the Depression, married women were not given jobs so I could not continue to teach had I wanted to do so.

We got along on Daddy's salary, $1140 a year. We had no telephone, no radio, no refrigerator, not even a clock. When we finally got a clock, I thought it was so wonderful to hear it tick. As for Daddy, he was very happy to have his own home.

Before we were married, Daddy lived with a Presbyterian lady who kept boarders. Bill Swalm came to Newville to preach a trial sermon and Mrs. McKean brought him to her house to eat. Bill and Daddy became good friends, instantly, shared interests and compared girlfriends. Bill got the preaching job, got married, moved to Newville. In spite of the great difference in our backgrounds, Alice and I also became good friends when I arrived a year later. It is the one Newville friendship we have continued through the years.

When Elaine was born, Daddy hit the clouds. She was a beautiful baby, pink like a rose. Daddy would carry her around and say over and over, 'Daddy's sugar, Daddy's sugar'. He was always a very willing father to help care for the children when the three of them were small. Because at that time I began having arthritis, it was hard to hang clothes on the line (there were no dryers). Daddy got up early each Monday morning. He filled the washer

*First home of Henry Hess Hackman and Minnie Becker
Hackman, Main Street, Newville, Cumberland County,
Pennsylvania.*

*Second home of Henry Hess Hackman and Minnie Becker
Hackman, 40 Parsonage Street, Newville, Cumberland County,
Pennsylvania.*

with water and helped to do the weekly laundry before he went to school.

Daddy is, and was, an activist. In those early years, war was threatening Europe again, and Daddy and Bill Swalm were both pacifists. They took part in, and sometimes organized, 'Peace Meetings' which did not always meet the approval of the Presbyterians for Bill or the school board for Daddy. I knew he was right, but I was afraid he would lose his job. He was also very active in persuading the town to float a bond issue in order to build a much needed addition to the school which would include a gym, shower rooms, and a new science laboratory.

Daddy's interest in the effort to keep our country out of the war which seemed to be threatening, lead him to join what was then called the Emergency Peace Campaign sponsored by the Friends, Mennonites, and Brethren. He went to Grinell, a Friend's College, for a brief training and then was sent with a team of three other young men to work in Ohio. Camp Sugar Grove was home base for their summer work. They did radio programs, spoke to service clubs, churches, etc. Daddy was so devoted to this cause that he said he felt as he left us at the farm, that there was the Divine Hand on the steering wheel of his car guiding him on his way.

The old saying, 'You can take the boy out of the country, but you cannot take the country out of the boy' can certainly be applied to Daddy. At 40 Parsonage Street, Newville, there was a little chicken house attached to the garage. One spring Daddy decided to get some chicks and raise chickens so we could have eggs. He kept the tiny chicks in the cellar until they were big enough to live out in the chicken house. Then he would hurry home for lunch at noon, let his pet chickens out to eat grass and scratch in the ground for a few minutes, then chase them back in again. Of course, he farmed an intensive garden.

We always spent our summers at the farm. Grandpa was very fond of apples. Pests were increasing, and the trees needed to be sprayed. Also Grandpa was getting older and was troubled with arthritis. It was hard for him to walk after the plow. So Daddy bought a John Deere tractor and a plow from the Newcomers in Mt. Joy. We all, except Grandma, went out in the field and followed as the agent demonstrated the way to use the plow. With a tractor Daddy could accomplish anything. Apple trees could be sprayed, and Grandpa could have piles of lovely apples.

We made cider and apple butter. Daddy sold some to the fraternity houses at the University of Pennsylvania when he was working on his master's degree. On Friday in the fall, we would pack up after school, go to the farm, make cider, go to Philadelphia on Saturday morning, back to Newville Saturday night or early Sunday morning and teach Sunday school.

Opening the fireplace and installing a cold water faucet in the kitchen so Grandma did not need to carry water from the pump were a few other things Daddy did around the farm. At this time, too, he became greatly interested in bees, and he had quite a large apiary at the end of Parsonage Street in an abandoned orchard. As always he developed this interest so well that he produced a great deal of honey which he sold to several stores. He won prizes at farm shows, and one year he took the sweepstakes at the Harrisburg State Farm Show.

Daddy had white rabbits for Bill which little Billy loved. Billy insisted on opening the door of the pen. I had to chase the rabbits around the yard and try to get them back in their pen.

We worked hard in the Brethren Church in Newville. It was an awfully ugly building for a church, and we had little in common with the people *there except that we all belonged to the human race and the Church of the Brethren. We had pressure put upon us from various people in the town at different times to join some of the 'better churches'. I think it was a result of our working as leaders in the early camp programs of the church which gave us a strong loyalty to the Brethren. At that time we met and worked with national church leaders who were fine and wonderful people. For several years we had responsibilities on committees at annual conference. These experiences showed us what the church could and should be, and, I believe, made a lasting impression on us. We helped to collect money by nickels, dimes, and quarters in the Newville Church. One Christmas vacation, we stayed at the farm, but Daddy went back and, with the young people, painted all the woodwork at the church. It was very cold so they took the shutters in the basement of our house and worked there. Later, a very nice family, Reeds, came to Newville, and we enjoyed working with them in the church.*

Early in the thirties a girl in camp, which was held at the end of summer school on the Elizabethtown College campus, wanted so much to go to high school, but she could not because she lived in the country near Quarryville, too far from the town. There was no transportation provided. Hazel Byers came to live with us and helped to do the housework. She graduated from Newville High School.

Another experience which affected our early life in Newville was having the Dan West family move into the other side of the house in which we lived. Dan had gone to Span during the Spanish Civil War to work in the relief program. His wife, Lucy, and their two children lived with us at that time. Their Joe and our Elaine were daily playmates which was very good. Our two families had the same values, and we could agree on methods of rearing our children.

So that Elaine would have more extended opportunities, I organized for a small fee, a kindergarten which met three times a week. Daddy had made two tables, one we left at the church at Newville. One is in the cellar at the Runnymede Farm. It was a good experience for Elaine because she had to share all of her toys. We had about ten children.

We were all rather surprised and excited when Daddy was invited to come to the college at Elizabethtown. It was very interesting to live on the college campus, and I enjoyed it very much. Daddy worked very hard. The war came. There were so few boys left at the college. Daddy wasn't needed. Grandpa was getting quite sick with asthma in addition to his arthritis. Daddy thought he liked high school teaching better than college teaching. There was a vacancy at Lititz where Daddy had always wished he could teach. So we moved to the farm. Daddy went to teach in the high school at Lititz. He took Elaine along to enter fourth grade there. Billy went to Grandma's at Sporting Hill. I went back to teaching, this time in the Union Square School, Rapho Township, Lancaster County, Pennsylvania. And that is the way it was!

But it was much, much more! Henry worked terribly hard on the farm. Getting up before dawn, he milked ten cows by hand; fed the pigs, chickens, and sheep; and bathed, dressed and drove the ten miles to school at Lititz. He worked in the fields far into the night. For several years, in addition to teaching school, he farmed the entire one hundred acre farm by himself.

As Elaine, Bill, and later John, grew older, they too learned the Hackman tradition of work. After school there were chores to be done: cows to fetch, chickens to feed, eggs to hunt, straw to throw down, the cow stable to sweep, the wood box in the kitchen to fill (there was no furnace) ashes to take out, homework to do, etc. On Saturdays, Bill helped his father at the barn and in the fields while Elaine usually worked in the house with her mother. Since Minnie also taught school, nearly all the traditional housework had to be done on Saturday. There was the huge lawn to mow (by hand!); the house to clean; clothes to wash, hang up to dry, sprinkle and iron; mending, flower beds to hoe and weed, etc. It was never a matter of getting done; it was only a matter of determining what should be done next.

Both extremely talented people, Henry and Minnie continue to leave their incredible mark upon society. Many people from all corners of the world have experienced the warmth and hospitality of their fireside. The church has grown and prospered because of their untiring loyalty and devotion. Young people have carried their teachings and influences down many and varied avenues of life. Conservation of natural resources is more clearly a reality because of their support and labor. But most important, they have passed on to their children and to their children's children the strength to face each new day with anticipation, assurance, and love. They have fostered in their children the desire to search for truth and to respond to it with integrity.

Henry Hess Hackman and Minnie Mae Becker Hackman had issue:

Dorothy Elaine Hackman, born 6 June 1934 Main Street, Newville, Cumberland County, Pennsylvania, died 23 June 1999. Married 7 June 1953 in the Palmyra Church of the Brethren, Palmyra, Lebanon County, Pennsylvania, Dorman John Grace, Jr., born 4 September 1933 Hershey Hospital, Hershey, Dauphin County, Pennsylvania,

Top row: Willard Henry Hackman, Dorman John Grace, Jr., Dorothy Elaine Hackman Grace. Bottom row: John Allen Hackman, Dorman John Grace III, Henry Hess Hackman, Minnie Mae Becker Hackman. Circa 1956.

son of Dorman J. Grace (21 May 1904 – 13 January 2002) and Mary Geib King (3 December 1908 – 12 November 1969), died 13 January 2004.

Willard Henry "Bill" Hackman, born 29 June 1938, 40 Parsonage Street, Newville, Cumberland County, Pennsylvania. Married 27 November 1958, Shelby Sensenderfer, born 11 October 1938, Manheim, Lancaster County, Pennsylvania, daughter of Fred Sensenderfer and Grace Demmy.

John Allen Hackman, born 19 May 1947, Runnymede Farm, Rapho Township, Lancaster County, Pennsylvania. Married 28 April 1973, Margaret Sue Yoder, born 28 February 1954, Goshen, Indiana, daughter of John Yoder and Elizabeth Hostetter. Divorced 22 April 1983, Lancaster County, Pennsylvania. Married 20 August 1983, Lancaster County, Pennsylvania, Joann

In 1973, Henry and Minnie Hackman deeded their Runnymede Farm in Rapho Township to their three children. Their youngest son, John, managed the farm. Henry and Minnie moved to his home on a neighboring farm, which was purchased by their children in Rapho Township, Lancaster County, Pennsylvania.

Tabor. Divorced 1992, Lancaster County, Pennsylvania.

Willis Hess Hackman and Mary Ebersole Martin Hackman had issue:[73]

Ray Donald Hackman, born 5 May 1933, married (1) Nellie R. (She became Mrs. Nellie R.

---

73 Mary Hackman letter, 1976, RD #3, Elizabethtown, Lancaster County, Pennsylvania. Letter held by Elaine Hackman Grace.

Brandt, Elizabethtown.[74]), married (2) 24 June 1972, Karen Ann Fortney, born 12 March 1949, daughter of Daniel Benjamin Fortney (born 23 January 1929, Harrisburg, Dauphin County, Pennsylvania, died May 1981) and Madeline Helen Ferranti, (20 May 1921, Corning, New York). Donald and Karen live at RD #3, Elizabethtown, Lancaster County, Pennsylvania.

Kenneth Lee Hackman, born 3 September 1934, married 4 February 1956, Marian Arlene Baker, born 29 January 1935, Conewago Township, Dauphin County, Pennsylvania, daughter of Paul M. Baker (20 September 1896 – 26 October 1969 of Conewago Township, Dauphin County, Pennsylvania) and Esther R. Aldinger (29 June 1900 – June 1985, Derry Township, Dauphin County, Pennsylvania). Kenneth and Marian live at RD #3, Elizabethtown, Lancaster County, Pennsylvania.

Annie Marian Hackman, born 20 November 1937, married 20 November 1959, Harold LeRoy McKain, born 25 September at Marietta, Lancaster County, Pennsylvania, son of Armor Leroy McKain (22 June 1906 – May 1990, Lancaster, Pennsylvania) and Helen Loretta Marley (29 June 1910 – November 1986, Marieta, Lancaster County, Pennsylvania). Marion and Harold live at 101 Fairview Avenue, Marietta, Pennsylvania.

Margaret Ann Hackman, born 11 March 1939, married 10 September 1960, John Kennedy Gill, born 3 October 1935, in Manchester, Lancashire, England, son of John Kennedy Gill (10 May 1901 – 13 October 1950 of Galashields, Scotland) and Margaret Ann Lomas (29 December 1899 of Manchester, Lancashire, England.) Margaret and John live at RD #4, Box 216, Elizabethtown, Lancaster County, Pennsylvania.

---

74 Engagement of Gerald A Hackman to Candace M Kraybill, Harrisburg Patriot News, 22 February 1977.

Alice Lorraine Hackman, born 6 February 1942, married 9 September 1976, John Henry Gerlach, born 21 January 1939 in Elizabethtown, Lancaster County, Pennsylvania, son of Paul Seigle Gerlach (29 February 1908 – April 1986) and Pearl Leah Brehm (13 October 1906 – August 1993). Lorraine and John reside at RD #1, Mount Joy, East Donegal Township, Lancaster County, Pennsylvania.

Willis Martin Hackman, born 8 January 1946, married 5 October 1968, Rosetta Brubaker, born 16 March 1949, daughter of Olin Winfield Brubaker (19 July 1920) and Gladys Rosetta Jaquish (1 February 1920). Willis and Rosetta live at RD #3, box 190, Elizabethtown, Pennsylvania.

Walter Hess Hackman and Margaret Bucher Boose Hackman had issue:[75]

Robert Lorin Hackman, born 20 October 1935, died February 1987, married 7 January 1956, Florence Mildred Stuber, born 5 February 1935 in Ephrata Township, Lancaster County, Pennsylvania, daughter of Harold Elwood Stuber (29 June 1913 – 19 June 1990 of Ronks, Lancaster County, Pennsylvania) and Esther Mohler (2 January 1912 – 13 December 2009 of Akron, Lancaster County, Pennsylvania.) Robert and Florence lived in Selinsgrove, Monroe Township, Snyder County, Pennsylvania.

Richard Hess Hackman and Betty Forney Hackman had issue:[76]

Betty Lou Hackman, born 27 May 1935, died 1 October 1991, married 24 June 1956, Thomas William Williams III, born 7 October 1935, Northampton County, Pennsylvania, son of Thomas

---

75 Margaret Hackman letter, 1976, 144 East Walnut Street, Ephrata, Lancaster County, Pennsylvania. Held by Elaine Hackman Grace.

76 Betty Hackman letter, 1976, RD #3, Lititz, Lancaster County, Pennsylvania. Held by Elaine Hackman Grace.

William Williams II, (Wind Gap, Northampton County, Pennsylvania) and Emma B. Bonser (Nazareth, Northampton County, Pennsylvania). Betty and Thomas lived at 711 East Millport, Leola, Lancaster County, Pennsylvania.

Richard Forney Hackman, born 24 January 1940, married 21 June 1969, Bonadine Marie Bucher, born 25 March 1945, Lebanon, Lebanon County, Pennsylvania, daughter of Samuel Bucher, born 27 October 1923, and Grace Snyder (4 February 1924 – May 1986). Richard and Bonadine live at 723 Owl Hill Road, Lititz, Lancaster County, Pennsylvania.

Robert Forney Hackman, born 10 September 1946, married 26 June 1970, Janice Marie Breneman, born 2 November 1948, Lancaster County, Pennsylvania, daughter of John Robert Breneman (4 March 1922 – 25 November 2006) of Elizabethtown, Lancaster County, Pennsylvania and Helen Marie Zimmerman (21 August 1921 – 25 August 1989) of Orwin, Schuylkill County, Pennsylvania. Robert and Janice live at 725 Owl Hill Road, Lititz, Lancaster County, Pennsylvania.

Violet Gertrude Hackman Pfaltzgraff and Roy Edward Pfaltzgraff had issue:[77]

Roy Edward Pfaltzgraff Jr., born 8 September, 1943, Philadelphia, Pennsylvania, married Kathryn Krehmeyer of Maxtun County, Colorado.

George Hackman Pfaltzgraff, born 22 April 1945, in Garkida, Nigeria, married (1) Cynthia Porter of Manchester, Indiana, and (2) Peggie of Cincinnati.

David Jasini Pfaltzgraff, born 11 September 1946, in Lasa, Nigeria, married Ruth Susanna Kehr of York, Pennsylvania.

---

77 Violet Pfaltzgraff letter, 1976, Garkida via Vola, Gongola, Nigeria.

Kathryn Joyce Pfaltzgraff, born 22 October 1953, in Lasa, Nigeria, married David A. Williford of Dandridge, Tennessee.

Nevin Mark Pfaltzgraff, born 13 November 1955, in Garkida, Nigeria, married Antonia Marie Parry.

Emma Amelia Hackman White and William Walter White II, had issue:[78]

Emily Faline White, born 16 February 1943, Lititz, Lancaster County, Pennsylvania, married 3 August 1943 at Elizabethtown, Lancaster County, Pennsylvania, Lawrence David Knorr, born 4 May 1943, son of George L. Knorr (6 March 1912 – 30 October 2001) of Mohnton, Berks County, Pennsylvania, and Alice R. Burnish (11 September 1911 – 3 July 2008) of Reading, Berks County, Pennsylvania. Emily and Lawrence live in Montevallo, Alabama.

William Walter White III, born 12 December, 1944, Lititz, Lancaster County, Pennsylvania, married Dorothy Krafft, born 1955. William and Dorothy live in Elizabethtown, Lancaster County, Pennsylvania.

---

78 Knorr, Lawrence, *The Relations of Milton Snavely Hershey, 4th Ed,* (Sunbury Press, New Kingstown, PA 2007), pages 163 & 223.

Generation VII

Dorothy Elaine Hackman met Dorman John Grace Jr., at Camp Swatara, Bethel, Pennsylvania, during the summer of 1950. Elaine had just turned sixteen; John was nearly seventeen. One evening for campfire, the girls were encouraged to ask the boys for dates. During this time, before women's liberation, a situation like this one was very unusual. Elaine volunteered to help out a shy girl friend by asking John to be the friend's date. It was an unkind act since she knew, by woman's intuition, that John was wishing she would ask him for herself. Not easily discouraged, John spoke for himself later in the week, and the courtship, which resulted in a beautiful life for both of them, began.

John was very active in Palmyra High School, Palmyra, Lebanon County, Pennsylvania. He took candid pictures for the year book and developed them himself. He sang in the glee club, participated in district and state choruses, played in the band, played football, . He was also active in church affairs (Palmyra Church of the Brethren), singing in the choir and participating in various youth activities. Elaine was sometimes annoyed by the fact that no dates could be scheduled for a Thursday night. Choir practice took precedence over any other activity. John graduated second in his high school class of about ninety.

Elaine attended Lititz High School, now Warwick, Lancaster County, Pennsylvania. At that time Rapho Township did not provide a high school for its students. Her father, Henry, taught chemistry and physics at Lititz High School and Elaine and Bill (brother) rode along to school with him. Later, Rapho Township joined the Mainheim Central School System, and Bill attended high school in Manheim. In school, Elaine was interested in dramatics, girl's basketball, band, chorus, where she sang tenor because there were not enough boys, and working in the library. Elaine graduated in the upper tenth of her class of about sixty, however, she was not an honor student because she failed to complete her father's chemistry course.

An individual with a mind of her own, Elaine disappointed her parents on several occasions by making important decisions they considered to be unwise. However, they wisely allowed their daughter to make her own decisions and to live with the consequences of her actions.

One of these occasions was the chemistry incident. From fourth grade through twelfth grade, Elaine attended the public school in which her father taught – Lititz. Always, she was reminded that she could receive fewer favors than the other children because her father was a teacher. The whole situation seemed, at the time, to have more negative factors than positive ones, although it was certainly not unpleasant to attend school with her father. Elaine found her father's chemistry class difficult. She had little aptitude and no interest in the subject. This was a lethal combination. Henry was determined his daughter would learn chemistry. Elaine was equally determined that she couldn't learn chemistry. At the end of the term, Elaine should have received a "D" for the course. Getting a "D" in any course was simply never done in the Hackman family. Henry was not about to accept the situation.

"No daughter of mine will get credit for chemistry knowing what you know!," he informed his daughter. "If you want credit for this course, you must write a term paper."

Having received few, if any, privileges during her school career because her father was a teacher, Elaine was not about to accept handicaps either. She refused to write the paper. Henry refused to give her credit for the course. The permanent records show 'incomplete.'

John entered Lebanon Valley College, Annville, Lebanon County, Pennsylvania, in the fall of 1951.

"A little high school girl can't expect to hold on to a college man," Minnie told her daughter, trying to prepare her gently for her first heart break.

Actually, the major storms in this courtship had occurred during the first year of dating, and the relationship was relatively stable by this time. John had a scholarship and worked part-time in his father's insurance office to finance his way through college. He was an excellent student and was extremely active in college activities. He graduated first in his class.

Elaine entered Elizabethtown College in the fall of 1952. She majored in elementary education the first semester. In October of her freshman year, she and John became engaged, and college life became almost unbearable. Curfew was 7:00 PM. Freshman initiation seemed stupid and childish. Whenever a girl left the dorm, she was required to sign out, stating her destination and her expected time of return. A college education was extremely important to Henry and Minnie. They wanted the best for their daughter, and the best included a college education. They were not receptive to the idea of Elaine's dropping out of school even though she knew that she would not complete four years. In view of these facts, Elaine decided the best way to leave school would be to flunk out. She found a great deal of satisfaction in becoming the 'problem child' for her professors. She enjoyed the extra attention and the concern they showered upon her. By the end of the first semester, Henry, Minnie and Elaine had agreed to compromise. Elaine would finish the first year at college, but would change majors to secretarial science, in anticipation of an office job after her June wedding.

Although Henry and Minnie were not convinced that marriage for the two nineteen year-olds was a wise choice, they nevertheless again allowed their daughter to make her own decision. Henry, and John's mother, Mary King Grace, went along with John and Elaine to the Lebanon County Courthouse where application was made for a marriage license. On 7 June 1953, Elaine and John were married in the Palmyra Church of the Brethren, Chestnut Street, Palmyra, Lebanon County, Pennsylvania by the Rev. Frank S. Carper and the Rev. Nevin H. Zuck.

Their first home was an apartment on the second floor of the Valley Trust Building on the square in Palmyra. It was a new apartment and cost $50 a month. Elaine began work in the insurance office just down the hall. John was a junior at Lebanon Valley College and continued to work in the office. Time was a most precious commodity for him. He meticulously scheduled each day with the precision of a surgeon to insure adequate work and study time.

In the winter of 1955, John and Elaine moved to 757 Willow Street, Lebanon, Lebanon County, Pennsylvania. John's father had an insurance office and travel bureau at this location. There was an apartment on the second floor. John and Elaine lived here rent free. They carefully saved the 'rent

Wedding of John Grace and Elaine Hackman, 7 June 1953.
From left to right: Henry Hackman, Minnie Becker Hackman
(parents of the bride), Elaine Hackman (bride), John Grace Jr.
(groom), Mary King Grace, D. J. Grace (parents of the groom).
Palmyra Church of the Brethren.

money' and ate a menu of hamburgers and hot dogs in order to save money for a home of their own.

John graduated from college in 1955. We worked in the insurance office at the Willow Street location and received his CPCU designation indicating he was extremely knowledgeable in casualty and property underwriting. He soon decided that selling insurance bought him little satisfaction, and he began to work in the accounting area of the insurance operation. Technically, he became employed by Richard Kreider, CPA, but in reality, he worked for his dad.

The first child arrives, bringing great joy to Elaine and John. Dorman John Grace III arrived in the fall of 1955. He was a very tiny baby, weighing only five pounds one and one-half ounces when he came home from the Good Samaritan Hospital,

Lebanon, Lebanon County, Pennsylvania. He was the first grandchild in the family.

In January, 1957, John became self-employed as an accountant. On 4 February 1957, John and Elaine bought the house at 230 East Oak Street, Palmyra, Lebanon County, Pennsylvania from Robert and Helen Hartz. Mr. Hartz has been principal at the Palmyra High School for many years. He had built the house in 1933 and his family had lived there ever since. He was willing to sell his home to John and Elaine for less than he had originally hoped because he felt sure that they would take good care of it. The total cost was $19,800. It was a big home, and since the Hartz children were all grown, Mr. & Mrs. Hartz felt a smaller place would be more practical for them.

By this time, John was interested in sitting for the CPA examination, but he had to receive special permission from Irving Yaverbaum, CPA of

This house at 230 East Oak Street, Palmyra, Pennsylvania, was purchased by John and Elaine Grace in 1957, from Robert and Helen Hartz.

Harrisburg, because part of his two year's practical experience had been spent in a self-employed capacity rather than in working for a CPA. Generally, an individual sitting for the CPA examination would have spent the entire two years working for a certified public accountant. Among the questions put to John was 'do you think you can pass the examination.' John responded affirmatively. Mr. Yaverbaum was impressed with John's sincerity and honesty and finally gave his consent. In November 1957, John went to Philadelphia for three days of testing. He passed all the areas of the test on his first attempt and received one of the three highest scores in the state of Pennsylvania. For this achievement, he and Elaine were awarded an all-expenses paid trip to the CPA Convention held at Pocono Manor the following spring. It was an absolutely delightful experience.

Two darling babies arrived less than a year apart --- Nancy in 1958, Kathy in 1969. When Nancy

D. John Grace III and Nancy Anne Grace, Christmas, 1968.

D. John Grace Jr. and Elaine Hackman Grace with their children: Nancy (held by her father), John III, (sitting between his parents), Kathy (held by her mother).

started kindergarten, Kathy attended nursery school. Their mother, Elaine, decided to take some college courses just for fun. She took an elementary art course at Lebanon Valley College, followed by another art course, followed by U.S. history, educational psychology, teaching of reading, etc. In no time at all, there were twenty-four credits completed at LVC.

Elaine decided, with so many credits completed at LVC in addition to the ones completed at Elizabethtown, to complete her college education. She transferred her LVC credits to Elizabethtown College because she had credits at Elizabethtown that could not be transferred to LVC. In the summer of 1967, Elaine received her BS degree in elementary education, cum laude. Because of the shortage of teachers, she had done her student teaching in-service in the Pine Street Building in the Palmyra Area School System. Now, she returned to

Keating Summit, Potter County, Pennsylvania, 1976.

the district to teach kindergarten in the Forge Road Building.

Keating Summit, Potter County, Pennsylvania, holds an important place in the lives of the members of the Grace family. In 1962, John and Elaine purchased some heavily timbered mountain land and some meadow land from Daniel McLaughlin for $10 an acre. In the ensuing years, John continued to purchase adjoining land until he had accumulated about 1000 acres. Many lovely Thanksgiving days and memorable New Year's Eves have been spent with friends and family at 'Keating' watching the snow fall slowly and silently on the mountain peaks while the Franklin stove threw plenty of warmth to all of those within reach. Summer, too, has had its delights. Hikes through the woods and over the logging roads, swimming in the lake, mowing the fields with the old Ford tractor, taking rides over the mountain in the 1951 Jeep, digging for bottles where in 1900, outhouses used to be, have all contributed their share to

D. John Grace Jr. enjoys the autumn beauty of the hills at Keating Summit, Potter County, Pennsylvania, 1976.

treasured memories. Of course, deer camp at Keating has been an important annual event for the male members of the family.

John began teaching accounting at Lebanon Valley College in 1958. By 1970, he was carrying a full-time teaching load and advising students, as well as operating his own accounting business at 110 West Chocolate Avenue, Hershey, Dauphin County, Pennsylvania. One of the students he found himself advising was Alfred Toronka, a student from Sierra Leone, Africa. Alfred had an academic scholarship, but his room and board were paid by his uncle, an official in the Sierra Leone government. When the pro-U.S. government was overthrown, Alfred's uncle was thrown into prison, and Alfred's financial support ceased. From January 1971 until May 1972, Alfred lived with the Grace family. John III very graciously and willingly shared his room with his Sierra Leone 'brother.'

Hallmark Baron Grace joined the family in April, 1972. "Barry" was a beautiful silver Persian cat. John and his daughters, Nancy and Kathy, enjoyed showing Barry at various cat shows in Pennsylvania, New York, Virginia, and Maryland. In 1973, Barry was honored in *Cat's Magazine* by being named the fifth best cat in the East. Later, Bessie and Betsy were added to the cat family.

By 1976, the children were nearly grown. John III was enjoying his senior year in astronomy at Penn State University, University Park, Pennsylvania. Nancy, majoring in medical secretarial science, was enthusiastic about her freshman year at Elizabethtown College, Elizabethtown, Pennsylvania. Kathy, a senior in Palmyra Area High School, was active in dramatics and excelling in her academic work. Andrea Pohl, a

From left to right: Nancy Grace, D. John Grace III, Kathy Grace. The children are in their choir gowns.

German exchange student, was spending a year with the family. John Jr., was busy with an expanding CPA practice as well as lending his time to the scouting movement in Lebanon County and his expertise to the Palmyra Area School Board. Elaine continued to teach (now second grade) in the Forge Road Building of the Palmyra Area School System.

Dorothy Elaine Hackman Grace and Dorman John Grace Jr., had issue:

Dorman John Grace III, born 27 October 1955, at Good Samaritan Hospital, Lebanon, Lebanon County, Pennsylvania, married Sandra Boale, born 21 May, 1958, daughter of Jesse Donald Boale (born 13 April 1928) and Estelle Rachelle Pine (born 26 April, 1931), 20 August 1977 in New Castle, Pennsylvania. The family was living at 757 Willow Street, Lebanon, Pennsylvania when he was born.

Nancy Anne Grace, born 30 August 1958, at the Good Samaritan Hospital, Lebanon, Lebanon County, Pennsylvania, married David L. Bogdonoff, born 15 September 1955, son of Harold and Miriam Bogdonoff, 22 May 1983 in Hershey, Pennsylvania. The family was living at 230 East Oak Street, Palmyra, Pennsylvania when she was born.

Kathleen Kay (Kathy) Grace, born 11 August 1959, at the Good Samaritan Hospital, Lebanon, Lebanon County, Pennsylvania. The family was living at 230 East Oak Street, Palmyra, Pennsylvania.

Willard Henry (Bill) Hackman met his wife, Shelby Sensenderfer, during their freshman year in Manheim Central High School, Manheim, Lancaster County, Pennsylvania. It was definitely not love at first sight; however, by their senior year, they had each taken a second look, and love began to bloom. Bill courted Shelby with flowers which he sometimes left in the car and forgot to give to her.

Wedding picture of Willard Henry Hackman and Shelby Sensenderfer, November 1958.

After high school graduation in 1956, Bill began his college work at Elizabethtown College. Shelby went off to the Reading Hospital School of Nursing, Berks County, Pennsylvania. Christmas 1957 they became engaged, and on Thanksgiving Day, 27 November 1958, at 6 PM, they were married in the

Elizabethtown Church of the Brethren by the Rev. Nevin H. Zuck. It was a beautiful ceremony.

Bill and Shelby set up a temporary home in the basement of Shelby's parents' home at 178 Grant Street, Manheim, Lancaster County, Pennsylvania. During the week, Shelby lived at the Reading Hospital; Bill commuted from the farm in Rapho Township, Lancaster County, Pennsylvania, to Elizabethtown College. Weekends they spent together in the basement apartment.

Shelby became a registered nurse in 1959. That summer, Bill's parents, Henry and Minnie Hackman, went to Oakridge, Tennessee, where Henry had a scholarship to pursue studies in the teaching of physics and chemistry. Bill and Shelby spent the summer on the farm. Bill worked at RCA and took care of the farm. Shelby worked at the Reading Hospital. They bought a house trailer and moved it to Penn State where Bill would continue his studies in electrical engineering in the fall.

The trailer was parked at 64 Woodsdale Park, State College, Pennsylvania. Shelby worked at Centre County Hospital. Bill studied. The summer following their first year at Penn State, Bill worked for RCA at their Camden, New Jersey plant. Shelby stayed in State College to continue her job there.

The second year at Penn State demanded just as much stamina as the first. This year, Shelby worked for a rather eccentric dentist, and Bill continued to study. By 1961, Bill graduated with honors from Penn State with a BS in Electrical Engineering. That summer, they moved again to the Sensenderfer home. Shelby went to summer school at Elizabethtown College to work on her BS degree in nursing. Bill worked for RCA at their Lancaster Plant.

The fall of 1961, they returned to Penn State where Bill, having been awarded a fellowship, began

From left to right: Christopher Allen Hackman and Michael Frederick Hackman, the sons of Bill and Shelby Hackman.

work on his master's degree. Shelby went back to work for the dentist and later in the year worked for a general practitioner in State College.

Bill received his master's degree in June of 1962. The trailer was moved to the Hackman farm at RD #2, Rapho Township, Lancaster County,

Pennsylvania. Bill and Shelby continued living in the trailer at this new location. Bill was hired by RCA for a permanent position. They had been impressed by his work the previous summers. Shelby worked part-time at St. Joseph's Hospital, Lancaster, Pennsylvania.

In 1968, Shelby went back to school and received her BS in Education in 1972. After thoroughly enjoying a period of employment at Lancaster General Hospital School of Nursing as a nursing instructor, Shelby became a school nurse in inner-city Lancaster. This job required a great deal of skill, understanding and compassion. To expand her education, she worked very hard during the summer of 1976 in the School Nurse Practitioner Program at the Hershey Medical Center, Hershey, Pennsylvania.

Bill continued to work at RCA in a responsible and demanding position. He served on the Manheim Central School Board of Directors. He helped his brother John on the farm when he was needed. He spent a considerable amount of time making beautiful improvements to his home.

Bill, Shelby, their sons, and their friends have enjoyed many happy and satisfying hours at their shore home in New Jersey. Boating, water skiing, fishing and tanning in the sun were a welcome change of pace from the rigors of everyday living.

Willard Henry Hackman and Shelby Sensenderfer Hackman had issue:

Michael Frederick Hackman, born 8 June 1964, married (22 December 1984) and divorced Dana Lynn McFarland.

Christopher Allen Hackman, born 24 September 1965, married Colleen Hollinger 6 August 1988.

John Allen Hackman was born after Henry and Minnie Becker Hackman moved to the Rapho Township farm. The farm had been originally

Michael Frederick Hackman and Christopher Allen Hackman.

purchased by Jacob Becker, Minnie Becker Hackman's great grandfather, in 1837.[79] It had been handed from one Becker generation to another until it finally became the home of Henry and Minnie Hackman. 'The Farm' holds precious memories for all of Henry and Minnie's family, but most significantly for John.

John writes:[80]

Perhaps some of my earliest memories are of Grandma and Grandpa Becker. Since I stayed with them at Sporting Hill, Lancaster County, Pennsylvania, during the daytime when Mother was teaching, they became almost a second set of parents. I would ride along with Grandpa to the mill in Manheim where he would buy chicken mash. He would pile full the trunk of his 1936 Ford, and

---

79 Deed held by Henry and Minnie Hackman.
80 Original copy held by Elaine Hackman Grace, 230 East Oak St., Palmyra, Pennsylvania.

sometimes he would tie two or more 100 pound bags on the front bumper. The corn he fed his chickens he would sometimes shell by hand. I used to try to help, but it was too much for my small hands.

In the house at Sporting Hill, Grandma kept about two or three small cars or trucks for me to play with. Most of the time I would play in the kitchen near the kitchen range. Sometimes Grandpa sat on the wood box or a kitchen chair. Then, as I was crawling around on the worn linoleum floor, he would sometimes trap me by clamping my neck between his legs.

Outdoors I would play with a little red express wagon. It was my 'truck.' In their backyard I had tracks worn in the grass from many trips going somewhere.

Grandma kept a green corduroy suit for me in case she wanted to go away. It was very special. It seemed, however, that going away usually meant going to a viewing or a funeral. Grandpa had already died at this time, so there were probably several friends or relatives that died during the time of the corduroy suit.

Ironically, Grandma became very ill during the summer I started first grade. I no longer needed her to care for me while mother was teaching. In September, 1954, Grandma died. I remember I went to live with the Wilsons for a week or so. I wanted to go home, but I couldn't. Then one evening, the Wilsons took me to Grandma's to go home with Mother and Dad. Mother was in Grandma's 'good room' going through some of Grandma's things. I couldn't believe my eyes! I could hardly look. Mother's face was very swollen. She knew I was afraid. I think I cried. I was afraid she was very sick and might die. But, of course, it was a severe reaction to the gold injections Mother had taken for her arthritis.

Runnymede Farm, Rapho Township, Lancaster County, Pennsylvania.

But the biggest thing in my childhood was the farm. After school, there were the regular chores: feeding the calves, sweeping the cow stable, and hunting the eggs. That wasn't always fun, but charing the cats with the help of the dogs certainly was. We must have had the wildest cats in the county.

There was always something happening on the farm. It seemed Dad was constantly making improvements whether he could afford them or not. There was adventure, dreaming, and discovery. Dad was always in a hurry – he wasn't interested in nonsense.

Because Dad was involved in many organizations requiring meetings, Mother and I spent many winter evenings alone together. We had a game called 'Fatty and Skinny.' It was a playful shoving match. She was Fatty and I was Skinny. We would push each other around the kitchen until her arthritic legs had had enough. It was great fun.

Although I remember growing up as being a happy time, there were moments of discipline, too. In seventh grade, I failed English for one report period. Seventh grade was a difficult time for me. However, difficult or easy, failing wasn't acceptable for Dad. He gave me the only spanking I remember, and in the process he split the antique pie board he was using as a paddle. Next, he picked up the very large pie board and finished the job. I didn't get A's in English after that, but I didn't fail either.

Two years later, I began participating in football and track at school. My experiences of the next four years in sports are very important to me. The success I had there was mostly due to the fact that Dad taught me how to work. That put me ahead of most of my peers from the start. By the time I graduated from high school, I was listed in four school track records and was named to the football league all-star team. The recognition was nice, but the actual moments of special achievement during the competition are far more important.

In September 1965, I began my college education at Elizabethtown College, Elizabethtown, Lancaster County, Pennsylvania. My goal was to graduate in 1970 from both Elizabethtown and Penn State University with bachelor's degrees in Liberal Arts and Electrical Engineering. It was a long road, but for the most part, I did enjoy learning. Perhaps the most important result of those five years was my largely expanded horizon of ideas and experiences. It is very difficult to verbalize the profound effect it had. And for those reasons, more than any other, I am very grateful that Mother and Dad always planned for my college education. Interestingly, when I was seven, I can remember anticipating going to college. The seed was planted at an early age.

In 1970, when I graduated from college, the nation was deeply involved in the Vietnam War. That spring was a very nervous time on university campuses. Violence and destruction were common as students demonstrated against the war. Innocent bystanders were killed by gunfire at Kent State University. I could have been an innocent bystander somewhere. Later that summer, I was drafted by the military to serve in the war. Since I am and was a conscientious objector to war and the military establishment, I served my two-year obligation at a boys' home in Goshen, Indiana. To cope with life at

Runnymede Farm, Rapho Township, Lancaster County, Pennsylvania. The old smokehouse and the spring house can been seen to the right of the house. Picture taken fall, 1976.

*Wedding of John Allen Hackman and Margaret Sue Yoder, 28
April 1973, Goshen Church of the Brethren, Goshen, Indiana.
From left to right: John Yoder, Elizabeth Hostetter Yoder
(parents of the bride), Margaret Sue Yoder (bride), John Allen
Hackman (groom), Minnie Becker Hackman, Henry Hess
Hackman (parents of the groom).*

the boys' home in Goshen was the most severe test I
have experienced.

However, on the brighter side, during the fall of
1971, I met Margaret S (Margie) Yoder at the Goshen
City Church of the Brethren. Over a period of time,
we began spending much time together. Then, the
late summer of 1972, we decided to get married
sometime in 1973.

During September 1972, Margie and I visited
Mother and Dad at home on the farm. For some time
I had been occasionally wondering if I might not be
happy as a farmer. It would be a giant step. As
Margie and I were on the farmhouse porch, I paused
and looked around as memories flashed back:
playing in the woods behind the house and in the
orchard, the old spring house, growing up in the

fields, the work, the pets, the belonging – the whole place was a part of me. It was so overpowering that I leaned against a porch post and cried for a few moments. In my heart, it was my home. It was my farm, and that is where I wanted to be. That is what I wanted to do. It was a very peaceful feeling.

Much happened during the next few months. Margie and I decided we would like to farm the family farm; a wedding date was set (28 April 1973); a partnership was formed between my brother, Willard H. Hackman and my sister, D. Elaine Grace, and me, known as Runnymede Farms; and a second farm was purchased.

On 28 April 1973, Margie's family and my family gathered in Goshen, Indiana for our wedding. For the most part, our families had not met prior to the wedding. There were many introductions, and everybody had a good time. After being one-half of the main attraction in our wedding, I decided that one wedding was definitely enough. The day after our wedding, Margie and I started home for the farm. Two days after our wedding, I was finishing the plowing for that year's corn crop.

Soon we will have been here four years. Sometimes I think of the generations within the family before us. We are the sixth generation to live in this house, to work on this farm. The roots are very deep. As Dad used to ask when I was a child: 'What would Grandpa Becker say if he could see how things are now.' I wonder what Grandpa, Great Grandpa, and Great Great Grandpa Becker would say.

Margie, a very young bride, found herself suddenly thrust into the most difficult role of farmer's wife. She responded with unbelievable understanding and energy. Now, in her second year of nurses training, she continues to be a

Runnymede Farmhouse. Picture taken in 1976. The house is actually made of logs, and the fireplace, which once heated the house, is still operational.

homemaker, an excellent cook, a versatile seamstress. She enjoys knitting, quilting, crewel embroidery, etc. (The couple divorced 23 April, 1983)

Ray Donald and Nellie Hackman had issue:

Dennis Ray Hackman, born 24 November 1953, Hershey, Dauphin County, Pennsylvania.

Gerald Allen Hackman, born 24 October 1954, Hershey, Dauphin County, Pennsylvania.

Randall Lee Hackman, born 10 December 1955, Hershey, Dauphin County, Pennsylvania.

Gary Jay Hackman, born 23 November 1957, Hershey, Dauphin County, Pennsylvania.

Cindy Lynn Hackman, born 16 March 1959, Hershey, Dauphin County, Pennsylvania.

Thomas Jon Hackman, born 29 June 1960, Hershey, Dauphin County, Pennsylvania.

Daniel Michael Hackman, born 16 January 1966, Corning, New York.

Tammy Sue Hackman, born 29 May 1969, Williamsport, Pennsylvania.

Terry Lee Hackman, born 29 May 1969, Williamsport, Pennsylvania.

Ray Donald Hackman and Karen Ann Forney had issue:

Rea Ann Hackman, born 15 July 1976, Elizabethtown, Lancaster County, Pennsylvania.

Kenneth Lee Hackman and Marian Arlene Baker Hackman had issue:

Brenda Kay Hackman, born 9 July 1956, Elizabethtown, Lancaster County, Pennsylvania.

Wanda Jean Hackman, born 8 December 1957, Elizabethtown, Lancaster County, Pennsylvania.

Kenneth Lee Hackman, born 31 January 1960, Elizabethtown, Lancaster County, Pennsylvania.

Annie Marian Hackman McKain and Harold LeRoy McKain had issue:

Tracy Louise McKain, born 24 May 1969, Lancaster, Lancaster County, Pennsylvania.

Sheila Nadine McKain, born 20 March 1971, Lancaster, Lancaster County, Pennsylvania.

Margaret Ann Hackman Gill and John Kennedy Gill had issue:

Terry Lee Gill, born 13 June 1961, Plattsburg, New York.

Tina Lynn Gill, born 3 August 1962, Lancaster, Lancaster County, Pennsylvania.

Dawn Marie Gill, born 24 July 1970, Lankenheath, England.

Alice Lorraine Hackman Gerlach and John Henry Gerlach had issue:

Carol Ann Gerlach, born 29 April 1965, Lancaster, Lancaster County, Pennsylvania.

Daryl Eugene Gerlach, born 19 December 1967, Lancaster, Lancaster County, Pennsylvania.

Douglas Scott Gerlach, born 10 April 1970, Lancaster, Lancaster County, Pennsylvania.

Willis Martin Hackman and Rosetta Brubaker Hackman had issue:

Tony Robert Hackman, born 20 March 1973, Lancaster, Lancaster County, Pennsylvania.

Robert Lorin Hackman and Florence Mildred Stuber Hackman had issue:

Karen Lee Hackman, born 2 August 1956, Ephrata, Lancaster County, Pennsylvania.

Steven Dean Hackman, born 26 Novemebr 1958, Ephrata, Lancaster County, Pennsylvania.

Betty Lou Hackman Williams and Thomas William Williams had issue:

Douglas Thomas Williams, born 26 June 1957, Lancaster, Lancaster County, Pennsylvania.

Donald Everett Williams, born 23 August 1959, Lancaster, Lancaster County, Pennsylvania.

Dee Ann Williams, born 28 July 1963, Lancaster, Lancaster County, Pennsylvania.

Robert Forney Hackman and Janice Marie Breneman Hackman had issue:

Amy Lynn Hackman, born 5 December 1970, Lancaster, Lancaster County, Pennsylvania.

Roy Edward Pfaltzgraff Jr. and Kathryn Krehmeyer Pflatzgraff had issue:
Renee Pflatzgraff
Rhonda Pfaltzgraff
Rebecca Pfaltzgraff
Roberta Pfaltzgraff

George Hackman Pfaltzgraff and Cynthia Porter Pfaltzgraff had issue:
Christine Catherine Pfaltzgraff

David Jasini Pfaltzgraff and Ruth Susanna Kehr Pfaltzgraff had issue:
Timothy David Pfaltzgraff
Michael Jasini Pfaltzgraff

Emily Faline White Knorr and Lawrence David Knorr had issue:
Lawrence Kevin Knorr, born 5 May 1964, Reading, Berks County, Pennsylvania, married (1) Shelly J Harris of West Lawn, Berks County, Pennsylvania, (2) Ann Louise Berger of Stony Creek Mills, Berks County, Pennsylvania, (3) Tammi Kay McCoy of Biglerville, Adams County, Pennsylvania. Lawrence and Tammi live on a Brethern-built farm near Churchtown, Cumberland County, Pennsylvania.
Alice Kathleen Knorr, born 11 August, 1965, Reading, Berks County, Pennsylvania, married Glenn Buchman of Kutztown, Berks County, Pennsylvania. Alice and Glenn live in Reading, Berks County, Pennsylvania.
David Brian Knorr, born 7 April 1968, Reading, Berks County, Pennsylvania, married Tara Phillips of Gulfport, Mississippi. David and Tara live in Gulfport, Mississippi.

William Walter White III, and Dorothy Krafft White had issue:
Shelby White
McKenzie White

Generation VIII

This generation, as of 2013, would certainly require another 40 pages or so to detail. At the time of this writing, there had not been time to follow-up on all of the additions. We are hopeful the updating of this book will prompt further discussions and submissions regarding the Hackman family and its ever-expanding tree. Following are the known Knorr children of the 8th generation:

Lawrence Kevin Knorr and Ann Louise Berger-Knorr had issue:

Taylor Berger-Knorr, born 22 June 1998, Reading, Berks County, Pennsylvania.

Lawrence Knorr with his very 'fashionable' daughters Taylor Berger-Knorr (left) and Abbey Berger-Knorr (right) relaxing at the Carlisle Country Club.

Abbey Berger-Knorr, born 4 May 2002, Reading, Berks County, Pennsylvania.

Both Taylor and Abbey live primarily with their mother near Carlisle, Cumberland County, Pennsylvania.

Alice Kathleen Knorr and Gary Fidler had issue:

Gary Kyle Buchman, born 30 April 1983, Reading, Berks County, Pennsylvania. Gary was subsequently adopted by Glenn Buchman.

Appendix

Susanna Hackman

Tracing the unknown widow of David Hackman proved to be a real challenge. Older family members recalled that she had remarried and had had a daughter who married a Bollinger. That was all.

David Hackman's will[81] named 'John Frantz, the brother of my mother-in-law' as executor. An 1831 arithmetic book[82] belonging to Samuel Brubacher listed the following: (a) 'Susanna Bear, Mary Bear, Elizabeth Bear, Fanny Bear, Ephriam Bear, Lea Bear, Isaac F. Bear was born 17 January 1815, David Bear.' (b) It listed conditions for the 'sale of goods and chattels' signed by John Frantz. (c) Also included among its pages was an 'inventory of the goods we have taken. Charles Rudy 51.33, Jacob Hummel 41.83, Susannah Hackman 30.00, Isaac F. Bear 33.65.'

Among the private papers to which we had access[83] we found a release for the donor of Catherine Brunner to Andrew B. Hackman. The release referred to 'all legal heirs and representatives of Fanny F. Bear: Jacob B. Judy, David B. Rudy, Sarah Rudy, Jacob B. Hackman,

---

81 David Hackman will Q 1 179, Lancaster County Courthouse, Lancaster, Lancaster County, Pennsylvania.

82 Samuel Brubaker arithmetic book, 1831, held by Henry H Hackman.

83 Materials held by Henry H Hackman, RD#2, Manheim, Lancaster County, Pennsylvania.

David B. Hackman, Andrew B. Hackman, Fanny Bollinger, Mary Rickert, John Bear, Gabriel Bear, Rolandis Martin, Wayne Martin.'

We concluded that David Hackman's widow was probably issue of a Bear – Frantz union. We methodically checked Lancaster County Courthouse records and discovered a 'John Bear having a widow named Anna and six children viz. Susanna intermarried with David Hackman, Mary intermarried with Samuel Brubaker (It was his arithmetic book which we mentioned in paragraph two on the previous page.), Elizabeth, Fanny, Leha, Isaac.'[84]

By 1 May 1847, Susannah had remarried. Her husband was now John Brubaker. 'I give and bequeath unto my son-in-law Charles Rudy, in trust however, and to... pay said interest from time to time as it accrues and comes to hand unto my daughter Susanna and her husband, John Brubaker... I do order and direct the said trustee Charles Rudy his executors or administrators to pay said share or portion unto the children of my said daughter Susanna, gotten by her present husband the said John Brubaker.'[85]

It appears that this is the same John Brubaker who was the widower of Catherine Hackman, the sister of David Hackman.[86][87]

Phares Gibble[88] shows John G. Brubaker married first to _____ Hackman and second to

---

84 Lancaster County Orphans Court record 1827, page 392, Lancaster County Courthouse, Lancaster, Lancaster County, Pennsylvania.

85 Anna Bear will, U 1 953, Lancaster, Lancaster County Courthouse, Lancaster, Lancaster County, Pennsylvania.

86 Jacob Hackman will, S 1 358, Lancaster County Courthouse, Lancaster, Lancaster County, Pennsylvania.

87 Misc. Book 1841, page 130, Lancaster County Courthouse, Lancaster, Lancaster County, Pennsylvania.

Susan Erb (nee Bear). We personally checked his records to see if we could determine his source for the Erb surname. We found the "Erb" added to his noted in pencil. There was no source listed. We believe that the surname "Erb" is in error. The only alternative to this assumption would be if Susanna married (1) David Hackman, (2) _____ Erb, and (3) John Brubaker. Time wise, this would have been possible, but difficult.

Susanna Bear Hackman Brubaker and John G. Brubaker are buried in the Hammercreek Cemetery, Lancaster County, Pennsylvania. They are buried with Grandmother and Grandfather Hackman, Anna Hackman, the daughter of David Hackman and Susanna Hackman, Susan B. Brubaker, Isaac Brubaker.

88 Phares Brubaker Gibble, *History and Genealogy of the Brubaker, Brubacher, Brewbaker Family in America* (Lititz: The Eastern Pennsylvania Brubaker Association, 1951), p. 74.

About the Authors

Dorothy Elaine (Hackman) Grace (1934-1999) was a great granddaughter of Andrew Baer Hackman, and a granddaughter of Willis Brenner Hackman (via Henry Hess Hackman).

"Elaine" is also the author of *The Becker Story*. She thoroughly enjoyed researching and writing about family history. Her life through 1976 is well chronicled in this work, including the connections to the family she loved so dearly.

Lawrence Knorr (1964-) is the 2nd great grandson of Andrew Baer Hackman, and a great grandson of Willis Brenner Hackman (via Emma Amelia Hackman). For those keeping score, this makes Lawrence a 'half-cousin once-removed' to Elaine.

Lawrence is the author of numerous other books including *A Pennsylvania Mennonite and the California Gold Rush, The Relations of Milton Snavely Hershey, The Descendants of Hans Peter Knorr, The Relations of Dwight D. Eisenhower, The Relations of Isaac F. Stiehly – Minister of the Mahantongo Valley, General John Fulton Reynolds – His Biography, Words and Relations* and *There is Something About Rough and Ready: A History of the Village at the Heart of the Mahantongo Valley.* He is the father of two beautiful daughters, Taylor and Abbey, and resides near Harrisburg, PA with his wife Tammi. Professionally, he is an Information Systems executive for Ahold USA, the grocery chain and was the Chief Information Officer for the Pennsylvania Liquor Control Board. He is also an accomplished graphic artist.

Lawrence holds a Bachelors Degree in Business & Economics (History Minor) from Wilson College and a Masters of Business Administration from the Pennsylvania State University. He is also a Project Management Professional and Certified Computer Professional. Lawrence teaches part-time as an adjunct professor at Harrisburg University and Wilson College.

Lawrence received an original copy of *The Hackman Story* from his grandmother Emma Amelia Hackman White in the early 1980's. It was this comb-bound 1976 edition that first prompted his interest in genealogy and family history. As he began researching his roots, Lawrence conversed via letters with Dorothy Elaine Hackman Grace.

"Elaine was always very encouraging," said Lawrence, "I looked forward to her updates and she to mine. I am very pleased to help present Elaine's work to a greater audience. I am certain she would be very proud of it."

www.ingramcontent.com/pod-product-compliance
Lightning Source LLC
LaVergne TN
LVHW091156080426
835509LV00006B/709